The World Economy: Trends and Prospects for the Next Decade

by Professor Sir James Ball
Professor of Economics,
London Business School

A special report for the BNAC's 25th Anniversary

BRITISH-NORTH AMERICAN COMMITTEE
Sponsored by
British-North American Research Association (UK)
National Planning Association (USA)
C.D. Howe Institute (Canada)

ISBN 0-902594-53-2
Published by the British-North American Committee

Produced in the United Kingdom
by Needhams Design & Print Ltd, London EC2

June 1994

Contents

Statement of the British-North American Committee to Accompany the Report

We expect economists to tell us what is likely to happen in the future; few go back to see what actually took place and how the predictions turned out.

The British-North American Committee is twenty five years old this year. At the start of its life, one of the Committee's founding members, the late Professor Harry Johnson wrote for it a study entitled "International Economic Questions Facing Britain, the United States and Canada in the 70s".

We thought it would be salutary to see what has happened in the world economy over the period and compare it to what we thought the issues were in 1969. At the same time we considered it would be useful to set down what seemed today to be the major problems facing the world economy in general and the United States, United Kingdom and Canada in particular.

We were singularly fortunate to have among our members Professor Sir James Ball. He readily agreed to the request of the Committee to undertake this task and we thank him for the thoroughness with which he has approached it. It is with Harry Johnson's text that Sir James starts.

His analyses of the past and his anticipation of issues which need addressing are lucid and challenging. He has not only provided the Committee with a full agenda for its future work but has also given to policymakers and others, a comprehensive framework for understanding something of the present complexities of the world economy.

We therefore commend this important study to a wider audience in the expectation that it will stimulate wide thought and discussion.

Members of the British-North American Committee Signing the Statement[1]

CO-CHAIRMEN

SIR DAVID PLASTOW
Chairman
Inchcape Plc
London

JOHN HEIMANN
Chairman
Global Financial Institutions
Merrill Lynch & Co. Inc.
New York, NY

CHAIRMAN, EXECUTIVE COMMITTEE

DAVID MORTON
Chairman
Alcan Aluminum Ltd
Montreal, Quebec

MEMBERS

LESTER A. AMEDEI
Senior Vice President
Texaco Refining & Marketing Inc.
Universal City, CA

N. WILLIAM ATWATER
President
Foster Wheeler International Corporation
Clinton, NJ

JOSEPH E. BAIRD
Dean Witter
Beverley Hills, CA

PROFESSOR SIR JAMES BALL
Chairman
Legal & General Group Plc
London

R.C. BASKEN
Executive Vice President
Communications, Energy and
Paperworkers Union of Canada
Ottawa, Ontario

ROBERT P. BAUMAN
Chairman
British Aerospace Plc
Farnborough, Hants

DAVID BEATTY
President
Weston Foods Ltd
Toronto, Ontario

MICHAEL BETT
Director
British Telecom Plc
London

ROGER BEXON
Chairman
Laporte Plc
London

CARROL D. BOLEN
Vice President
Director, Speciality Plant Products
Pioneer Hi-Bred International, Inc.
Des Moines, IA

WILLIAM BRADFORD
President & COO
Dresser Industries Inc.
Dallas, TX

MARTIN BROUGHTON
Deputy Chairman & Group Executive
BAT Industries Plc
London

---

[1] Membership on the Committee does not necessarily signify agreement with all the contents of its publications.

TOM BURLISON
Deputy General Secretary
G.M.B.
London

DOMINIC CADBURY
Executive Chairman
Cadbury Schweppes Plc
London

SIR PETER CAZALET
Chairman
APV Plc
London

SAMUEL F. CHEVALIER
Vice Chairman
The Bank of New York
New York, NY

SIR ROBERT CLARKE
Chairman
United Biscuits (Holdings) Plc
Isleworth, Middlesex

SIR ANTHONY CLEAVER
Chairman
AEA Technology
London

MARSHALL A. COHEN
President and Chief Executive Officer
The Molson Companies Ltd
Toronto, Ontario

ALBERT J. COSTELLO
Chairman & CEO
American Cyanamid Company
Wayne, NY

PROFESSOR SIR FREDERICK CRAWFORD
Vice Chancellor
Aston University
Birmingham

SIR GRAHAM DAY
Hantsport, Nova Scotia

BARONESS DEAN OF
THORNTON-LE-FYLDE
Chairman
The Independent Committee for the Supervision of Standards of Telephone Information Services (ICSSTI)
London

JEAN-CLAUDE DELORME
Chairman and CEO
Caisse du depot et placement du Quebec
Montreal, Quebec

RICHARD DULUDE
Vice President
Corning Incorporated
Corning, NY

HON J. TREVOR EYTON
Chairman
Brascan Limited
Toronto, Ontario

MAUREEN FARROW
Executive Vice President
Loewen, Ondaatje, McCutheon Ltd
Toronto, Ontario

PROFESSOR EDWARD A FEIGENBAUM
Professor of Computer Science
Stanford University
Palo Alto, CA

WILLIAM B. FINNERAN
Chairman
Edison Control Corporation
New York, NY

HON. ALASTAIR W. GILLIESPIE
Chairman
National Westminster Bank of Canada
Toronto, Ontario

DON J. GUNTHER
President
Bechtel Group, Inc.
San Francisco, CA

HON. ALEXANDER M. HAIG JR.
President
Worldwide Associates Inc.
Washington, DC

RONNIE HAMPEL
Deputy Chairman & CEO
ICI Plc
London

G. R. HEFFERNAN
President
G.R. Heffernan & Associates Ltd
Toronto, Ontario

PAUL J. HOENMANS
Executive Vice President
Mobil Oil Corporation
Fairfax, VA

SIR SIMON HORNBY
Chairman
Lloyds Abbey Life Plc
London

ROGER HURN
Chairman
Smiths Industries Plc
London

DONALD P. JACOBS
Dean
J L Kellogg Graduate School of Management
Northwestern University
Evanston, IL

JOHN T. JOYCE
President
International Union of Bricklayers
& Allied Craftsmen
Washington, DC

THOMAS E. KIERANS
President and CEO
C.D. Howe Institute
Toronto, Ontario

SIR JOHN KINGMAN
Vice Chancellor
University of Bristol
Bristol

PAUL KOFMEHL
Chairman
Franklin Health Group Inc
Ramsey, NJ

SIR RICHARD LLOYD
Deputy Chairman
Hill Samuel Bank Limited
London

PIERRE LORTIE
Chairman
Bombardier Capital Inc.
Montreal, Quebec

MALCOLM R. LOVELL, JR.
President and CEO
National Planning Association
Washington, DC

DR PAUL MACAVOY
Dean
William Brothers Professor
in Management Studies
Yale School of Organization & Management
New Haven, CT

WILLIAM A. MACDONALD
President
W A Macdonald Associates Inc.
Toronto, Ontario

DAVID MCKINNEY
Senior Vice President
IBM Corporation
New Cannan, CT

JOHN MCNEIL
Chairman & CEO
Sun Life Assurance Company of Canada
Toronto, Ontario

GEORGE W. MALLINCKRODT
Executive Chairman
Schroders Plc
London

PHILIP A. MARINEAU
Executive Vice President
The Quaker Oats Company
Chicago, IL

SIR COLIN MARSHALL
Chairman
British Airways Plc
Hounslow, Middlesex

RICHARD L. MEASELLE
Managing Partner
Arthur Anderson & Co.
Chicago, IL

JOHN MILLER
Trustee
National Planning Association
Sandy Spring, MD

WILLIAM R. MILLER
New York, NY

SIR GEOFFREY MULCHAY
Executive Chairman
Kingfisher Plc
London

NEIL SHAW
Chairman and Chief Executive
Tate & Lyle Plc
London

MRS STEVE SHIRLEY
Life President
F.I. Group Plc
Amersham, Bucks

CLINTON SILVER
Deputy Chairman & Managing Director
Marks and Spencer Plc
London

SHERWOOD H. SMITH, JR.
Chairman and CEO
Carolina Power and Light Company
Raleigh, NC

DR. MICHAEL D. SOPKO
Chairman and CEO
Inco Limited
Toronto, Ontario

WILLIAM W. STINSON
Chairman and CEO
Canadian Pacific Limited
Montreal, Quebec

JAN H. SUWINSKI
Executive Vice President
Opto-Electronics Group
Corning Incorporated
Corning, NY

PROFESSOR THOMAS H. B. SYMONS
Vanier Professor,
Trent University and Director,
Celanese Canada Inc.
Peterborough, Ontario

ALLAN R. TAYLOR
Chairman and Chief Executive Officer
Royal Bank of Canada
Toronto, Ontario

JONATHAN TAYLOR
Chairman
Booker PLC
London

ALAN TUFFIN
Immediate Past President
Trades Union Congress
London

WILLIAM I.M. TURNER
Chairman and CEO
Exsultate Inc.
Montreal, Quebec

JOHN A. URQUHART
Vice Chairman, Enron Corporation
President, John A. Urquhart Associates
Fairfield, CT

DEREK WANLESS
Director; Group Chief Executive
National Westminster Bank Plc
London

VISCOUNT WEIR
Chairman
The Weir Group Limited
Glasgow, Scotland

ALAN WHEATLEY
Director
N M Rothschild & Son Ltd
London

L.R. WILSON
Chairman, President & CEO
BCE Inc.
Montreal, Quebec

MARGARET S. WILSON
Chairman and CEO
Scarbroughs
Austin, TX

HUMPHREY WOOD
Chairman
Vinten Group Plc
London

STEPHEN P. YOKICH
Vice President
General Motors Department
Detroit, MI

LORD YOUNGER OF PRESTWICK
Chairman
The Royal Bank of Scotland Plc
Edinburgh, Scotland

Acknowledgements

I am indebted to the membership of the British-North American Committee which, in plenary session, and on an individual basis, has modified my early drafts, saved me from some errors, and added to its content. It would be invidious to single out names. It should be clear that I am responsible for the views expressed, and the errors and omissions that remain.

I would also like to thank Kathy Hammond for research assistance, and my secretary, Juliet Smith, who was responsible for the preparation of the text throughout.

The World Economy:
Trends and Prospects for the Next Decade
by
Professor Sir James Ball

EXECUTIVE SUMMARY

In 1969, the British-North American Committee was formed from among the leaders of the private sector of the United Kingdom, United States and Canada - drawn from business, banking, labour and academia. Its purpose is to promote better understanding between the countries by sponsoring objective studies on issues which seemed important to its members.

At the outset, the Committee commissioned one of its members, the late Professor Harry Johnson, to review the issues which he thought would concern us for the remainder of the century. This current study re-examines Harry Johnson's work and sets out the concerns that are likely to have to be addressed as we move into the next millennium.

Many of the issues that concerned us twenty five years ago are still with us today. Among them are the international monetary and trading system, the internationalisation of business, and the struggle to balance government spending and revenues. Harry Johnson did not anticipate either the inflationary surge of the 1970s & 1980s triggered by the oil price rise or the rise of Japan as a major economic player or the problems of unemployment. He did predict the end of the Bretton Wood arrangements for exchange rates and emphasised that world economic expansion would be made possible only as far as world trade rules were liberalised.

The main economic events of the last quarter century are reviewed and a number of issues are identified that, "whatever the longer term political outcome, are likely to present problems over the next decade".

International Trade

The paper argues that at no time since the second world war has the principle of free trade been under such threat. The widespread use of non-tariff barriers has tended to offset the advantages gained from successive GATT rounds. A warning is given that arguments for "managed trade" based on strategic trade theory will be heard increasingly. It is expected that trade is likely to be developed in part within the framework of trading groups such as the European Union and North America. The rise of the Asia Pacific region poses problems for Japan especially as there are likely to be increased links between China and the diaspora Chinese.

Inflation and the International Monetary System

Growth in international trade requires an efficient and stable exchange rates and low inflation. Domestic deregulation of financial markets across the world has resulted in increasing mobility of capital which will have a beneficial effect in the world economy. The control of inflation is the crucial condition necessary for financial stability. While low inflation is a policy objective of most OECD countries, it has not been without the cost in the form of higher normal unemployment rates. However, the upward pressures on public spending will ensure that deflation and falling prices will not recur but a return to the price inflation rates of the 1950s & 1960s is likely. Nevertheless, it is predicted that international monetary stability will remain a critical issue for the international trading world.

Employment

Unemployment levels began rising in the late 1960s and accelerated after the oil price shocks of 1973. It is now at levels which are considered to be unacceptably high. Labour market rigidities account for some of this, rapid rises in technology - driven productivity rates too, play their part and business structure changes suggest a continuing diminishing role for semi-skilled and unskilled workers in manufacturing industry throughout OECD countries in the next decade. The effects of this will be felt in both the social life of nations and in increasing demands for some policies to alleviate the problem.

Public Finance and the Role of the State

The role of governments as taxers and spenders has and will continue to increase while in a number of cases the role of government as managers is declining. Government "take" as a proportion of GDP has risen steadily in most countries and indebtedness by both state and private sector (personal and corporate) is dangerously high. There is no prospect of demands on the public purse diminishing and revenues are not buoyant enough to meet current requirements; the growing longevity of the population can only exacerbate the problem. A process of rebalancing the relationship between the individual and the state is inevitable and privatising the use of resources is the only way to address the issue.

The state's role of regulator will therefore be enhanced as its role as provider diminishes. This will be seen increasingly in such areas as environmental protection. "The danger is that the environmental lobbies supported by government regulation will impose costs on economic activity that in the long run will turn into a major social loss of welfare. This issue presents a serious problem for business, governments, and communities at large both now and in the foreseeable future".

The Behaviour of Nations

The apparent ending of a coherent threat from Communism in the East, associated with the reunification of Germany, raises the whole question of the need for the Pax Americana, and the willingness of America to provide it. A lurch toward isolation by the United States would be a serious matter for the world and ultimately for the United States itself. A retreat into the economics and politics of the inter-war period would be an unmitigated disaster for all. There are good reasons to assume this will not happen but that economic co-operation between nations is likely to become more difficult because what are seen as domestic needs will tend to dominate collective responsibility. What may be expected is "a rough ride along an uneven path".

The Pattern of Nations (The Developing World)

A close examination of data suggest that the share of the world output by G7 countries relative to that of developing countries may be grossly exaggerated. (It maybe below 50%). It is probably that non-OECD countries' share of world output will increase rapidly into the next century. This is partly because in all parts of the world there is emerging a new philosophy which encourages enterprise and economic freedom though the pace of change differs in each country. Such developments do not come easily and major countries fear increased competitiveness and protection will become more popular. It is therefore necessary to go on emphasising the benefits of free trade and multilateralism.

The most significant overall development in the next decade in economic terms will be the continual growth and expansion of Asia including China and India. Early next century China could become the second largest economy in the world after the United States; only political events could prevent this.

Conclusion

Rapid economic growth, similar to that of the past will not be repeated. The path of technology will create problems of labour market adjustment for industrial countries particularly the European Union. Countries outside the OECD will increase their share of world output and trade which is a desirable and normal course of events. It will generate increasing protectionist and isolationist tendencies which must be resisted as the political as well as economic consequences will be disastrous. Inflation will stay subdued unless an unanticipated shock happens. Pressures to enlarge public provision of services, and therefore of taxes, will require a radical shift in how these services are delivered and financed.

The ending of the Cold War has, at best, demonstrated the superiority of the market system over collectivism. Some form of managed capitalism is likely to become the future pattern.

1. Prologue

1994 sees the 25th Anniversary of the British-North American Committee. It was founded by a group of British, American and Canadian business people, trade unionists and academics. Its initial concern was to promote a clearer understanding of the economic opportunities and problems facing the three countries. At the outset it declared that:

> "It believes that sound relations between these three countries in the context of an increasingly interrelated world are essential to future prosperity and seeks to promote better understanding through the collection of facts and their widespread dissemination."[1]

In serving these aims, the Committee planned to sponsor a series of objective studies to be undertaken by qualified experts which, with the Committee's approval, would be published. On the basis of these studies and discussion at its semi-annual meetings, the Committee Members from time to time expected to communicate their views on policy issues arising to their respective governments and to the public at large.

Since that inception, the Committee has realised the aims of its founders. The Committee has sponsored and published some forty studies by distinguished experts and practitioners covering a wide variety of relevant topics. They have included studies of the international monetary and trading system, problems of employment and labour markets, fiscal problems and other issues relating to international business, economic development and many more. It pioneered early discussion of the environment in relation to business and the importance of infrastructure to business in general. In addition, the Committee has published "issue" studies on topics such as education and training and the international financial system as well as a number of occasional papers prepared by members of the Committee themselves.

---

[1] BNAC Mission Statement. New York City, December 1969

At the outset of the Committee in 1969, the members asked the late Professor Harry Johnson (a member of the Committee) to prepare a paper presenting his personal views of the international economic problems likely to be of special interest to the Committee over the following decade, which was subsequently published. On the occasion of the 25th Anniversary of the Committee this paper returns to many of the questions raised by Harry Johnson a quarter of a century ago and looks forward to the issues that we may expect to concern the membership of the Committee into the next century.

It differs in scope and focus from Johnson's earlier essay in two significant respects. The first is that it is difficult to sustain the optimism of the founding fathers that the relationship between the three English speaking countries would remain of such significance as it appeared twenty-five years ago. Johnson did recognise the prospect of the UK becoming a member of what is now the European Union and the difficulties that might emerge in relations between the UK and North America in general. For these reasons, if for none other, the future of the three countries must be put into a total world context rather into a parochial framework that focuses on the three countries alone. Secondly, while Johnson foresaw a major shift in the nature of international business with a major extension of the role of multinational enterprises ("trans-national" corporations he called them) he could hardly have foreseen the extent to which the integration of trade and financial markets through de-regulation has bound countries together. The consequence of this is that it is virtually impossible to draw a clear distinction between economic problems that are "international" as contrasted with those that are "domestic". It is for both these reasons that the word "world" occurs in the title of this paper. What are relevant to the members of the Committee are world issues.

The paper proceeds as follows. Firstly, we take a brief look at the world as Harry Johnson foresaw it and how that vision turned out. Secondly, we then consider on a broad canvas how the world background has changed. Given that background, we deal with what this paper regards as the central economic issues *seriatim*. Finally, the paper essays some thoughts on the implications of these issues for the economic framework within which we might expect to do business in the foreseeable future.

2. The World in 1969 and After

When Harry Johnson wrote in 1969, the world was approaching the end of an era. The post-war economic world rested formally in large part on the Bretton Woods Agreement that created a framework for financial stability in the West. Politically and economically, through the early post-war period, the 1950s and into the 1960s, the Western world depended on the strength of the US economy and the Pax Americana. The formal ending of the old Bretton Woods system in August 1971 when President Nixon suspended the convertibility of the dollar into gold signalled a major shift in the balance of economic power that had been taking place over the previous decade. Despite this change, the Pax Americana lived on, but the world entered into a period of economic instability relative to the quarter of a century after the war that is with us still.

Given his brief, Johnson inevitably focussed on the issues of the international monetary system and trade. He clearly anticipated the coming problems with the Bretton Woods arrangements.

> "In the short-run, there is every sign of an approaching dollar crisis in the sense of a return to large US balance of payments deficits and the unwelcome necessity for other countries to finance these deficits by accumulating dollars on a large scale. The dollar is clearly overvalued in relation to the other major currencies and an adjustment of the exchange rates among them will have to be made at some point".[2]

The adjustment of course did not come for another two years, but when it did, it swept away the anchor of financial stability. Johnson speculated that the central issue for the next decade would be the substitution of Special Drawing Rights for the US dollar, thus providing an alternative source of international liquidity. This in fact did not come about for two reasons.

---

[2] Harry G Johnson. "International economic questions facing Britain, the United States and Canada in the 70's", *BNAC Paper No 1*. June 1970 p. 5

The first is the technical one, that after the collapse of the exchange rate mechanism within the Bretton Woods Agreement, the world, and most notably the United States, suddenly became enamoured of floating rather than pegged exchange rates. In 1969, Johnson still believed that the maintenance of international financial stability depended on contriving

> "... some means of rendering the monetary policy of the Federal Reserve system more responsible and responsive to the requirements of the international economy as a whole and less subordinate to the purely domestic requirements of the United States." (Johnson *op cit* p.6)

But after 1971, and up until the middle of the 1980s, successive US administrations took refuge behind a floating dollar, which, in theory, if not in practice, insulated US monetary policy from the external world and conversely. Interest in creating a new dollar substitute and indeed interest in wholesale international monetary reform simply disappeared and in the brave new world commitment to floating rates became as complete as the prior commitment to pegged rates, until in the European Community, interest was refocussed by the establishment of the ERM in 1979.

The second reason why the monetary issues did not turn out quite as Johnson expected was something that he would not have reasonably foreseen, namely the rise in the price of oil, and its impact on both the world trading and monetary system. But material as the two oil price increases of the 1970s were in influencing the actual paths of inflation and economic growth in the major countries, Johnson foresaw that the decade before him was to present new problems on the international monetary front that had largely been contained since the Second World War. As we shall see later, those problems are still with us and have yet to be resolved.

There is little doubt that the liberalisation of trade, culminating in the so-called Kennedy Round of tariff reductions begun in 1964, played a central role in encouraging growth and prosperity under the financial umbrella of the Bretton Woods exchange rate agreement. Indeed, Johnson in 1969 went as far as to say that:

> "The Kennedy Round may be said to have virtually completed the achievement of the objectives for the world economic system embodied in the conception of the General Agreement on Tariffs and Trade, in the sense that it has established for the 1970s a regime of

> relatively free trade with exceptions generally agreed to lie within the purview of national sovereignty." (Johnson *op cit* p.7)

For Johnson, the only serious question that remained was, that

> "If a further freeing of world trade is accepted as being a desirable objective, the question arises as to the best strategy for pursuing it." (Johnson *op cit* p.8)

There is no serious discussion in Johnson's essay as to whether the pursuit of free trade might not be a desirable objective. The way forward was seen as one of choosing the most appropriate negotiating tactics, culminating possibly in some multilateral free trade association among those advanced nations that were willing to pursue the free trade objective. There were indeed seen to be some problems on the horizon, prophetically including the question of non-tariff rather than tariff barriers to trade, with which we have become increasingly acquainted over the last twenty years. Johnson correctly predicted that:

> "As explicit tariff barriers fall as a result of the Kennedy Round agreements, non-tariffs barriers to trade are likely to become more of an issue in international economic relations, and private non-tariff barriers in particular are likely to come in for censure, informed or ill-informed as such censure may be." (Johnson *op cit* p.9)

It was also recognised that a re-allocation of resources as a result of tariff reductions might require the provision of adjustment costs for displaced firms and workers. And to demonstrate why it is often said that in economics the questions remain the same, it is merely the answers that change, consider the following observation on, and concern about, the fact that while protectionism in industrial products had declined in Johnson's time, this had not been so in agriculture.

> "A major problem of the 1970s will be to unwind the agricultural protectionism that has been built up in the developed countries over the past half century on the basis of the joint myths of the need for national self-sufficiency in food and the strategic importance of food as an economic commodity, and to replace it by policies that direct themselves to the real economic problem,

> which is to relieve the poverty of the farm population and to transfer resources from agriculture into industrial pursuits." (Johnson *op cit* p.11)

In the context of the discussion of the Uruguay Round, one can only observe that some things never change.

Johnson was also concerned with the process and financing of economic development. At his time of writing, he noted the disillusion of the major economies towards fulfilling the ambitious objectives of aid giving and the opening of domestic markets to the developing countries. He predicted that the future of the developing countries had to depend less and less on official foreign aid and more and more on the opening of markets for manufactures by the advanced countries and an increase in private investment in developing countries. He recognised the tensions that would arise between the old and the new industrial countries. But the pattern that development took was clearly (and reasonably) not foreseen. Johnson's paradigm like that of many other contemporary economists was one of agriculturally based societies struggling to re-allocate resources between primary and secondary production. What was not foreseen was the creation of industrial competitive advantage that has resulted in the economic success of Japan and the Newly Industrialising Countries, producing one of the main sources of tension in the modern trading world. Indeed it is a sign of times changing that in the whole of Harry Johnson's essay Japan gets not a single mention!

Johnson clearly anticipated the sort of problems that might arise between the UK and North America as a result of UK membership of the European Community and the generally deleterious effects of the Common Agricultural Policy. He was correctly pessimistic about the willingness of the Europeans to do anything about it other than,

> "... a reduction in the lavishness of the previous price supports ... and very likely ... the uneconomic generation of surplus in Europe will continue .. and North America will suffer sharp losses of agricultural export markets. Given the "Green Revolution" in the less developed countries, there are likely to be continuing tensions over access to the European market on the one hand and over the disposal of agricultural surpluses as development aid and in commercial markets elsewhere in the world." (Johnson *op cit* p. 17)

He also opined that

> "In a world divided along geographical lines into trading blocs, Canada would be under strong economic pressure to seek free trade with the United States ..." (Johnson *op cit* p. 18)

Finally Johnson identified a number of specific issues that he thought were common to the three countries, that included the state of public finance, education, poverty and the problems of cities. He was concerned with a problem that seriously affects all the three countries today.

> "One obvious problem for the 1970s will be that of public finance and taxation. On the one hand, in all three countries the prospective growth of demand for government services and therefore for tax revenue to finance governmental expenditure on the provision of the services is awesome. On the other hand, in all three countries there are plans, in various stages of readiness for implementation, for the improvement of the tax system and the removal or mitigation of its adverse effects." (Johnson *op cit* p. 21)

The events of the 1970s it turned out both aggravated and postponed many of the issues here until the following decade. The history of fiscal policy in the three countries over the last decade is a stark manifestation of much of what Johnson feared.

The purpose of this review has not been to assess Harry Johnson's prescience about the future. It is meant to do two things.

The first is to provide some starting point to assess how the world has developed since 1969. There remains in Johnson's essay, some of the optimism that characterised the economic world in the first quarter century after the Second World War. There were problems to come. The world economic order would need to be changed, particularly in the light of the relative shift in economic power between the United States and the rest of the World, notably at that stage Europe and Japan. But reading between the lines, one suspects that Johnson thought that rational behaviour would probably permit evolution without drama as far as the world economy was concerned. There is no serious discussion in the essay of inflation (the scourge of the 1970s and early 1980s) or of the problems of unemployment (the major concern of the 1980s and into the 1990s).

The second is that reading Johnson today we should note how many of the issues that concerned him twenty-five years ago are still with us in one form or another. The international monetary and trading system absorbs much of our attention. As Johnson saw, if imperfectly, business would become increasingly international. The struggle to balance the public purse, to bring government spending and revenue into line in the major industrial countries would become an increasingly uphill task. These observations underline the apparently intractable and recurring nature of many of the problems we face today, that are discussed below. Re-reading Johnson's observations at the outset of the BNAC should engender a note of caution as to how difficult it is to deal with them.

3. The World As it Has Been

Many events have conspired to determine the behaviour of the economic world throughout the life of the BNAC, some anticipated by Harry Johnson and some not. We argue here that while many may be listed, the principal factors that have shaped the world economy in the last quarter of a century have been the ending of the exchange rate system as practised under the banner of Bretton Woods, the increases in oil prices in the 1970s (and their decline in the late 1980s), the emergence of the United States large fiscal deficit in the early 1980s, and the end of the Cold War. Before turning to a series of specific issues that relate to the rest of this century and beyond, it is worth pausing for a moment to see where we are coming from. As has already been suggested, many of the problems we face did not appear yesterday. They are rooted in both the immediate and the more distant past.

The immediate consequence of the suspension of the convertibility of the dollar into gold in 1971 was to remove the anchor that had guaranteed international stability in terms of stable nominal exchange rates and low inflation. At the outset, these benefits were secured by pegging exchange rates to the dollar which was in turn tied to gold. Since, under this system world monetary policy was effectively US monetary policy, low inflation for the world as a whole was a function of how US monetary policy was conducted (although high rates of inflation were experienced in some of the developing countries). While the end of the system was probably inevitable, its death was hastened by the Vietnam War and a major outflow of dollars from the United States. The US could no longer play the role of custodian of the world's inflation rate to the satisfaction of the rest of the world.

The operational consequence of the change was to return the responsibility for monetary policy to individual countries. This development was much misunderstood by economists, politicians, civil servants and business alike (including in passing the author of this paper, but not by the late Harry Johnson). The misunderstanding lay in the fact that while governments correctly saw that they now had control, and needed in a sense to pay no attention to the dollar, they misunderstood what they in fact needed to control. The early 1970s saw a significant pause in economic activity and a general rise in unemployment, coincidentally with the end of Bretton Woods. Policy-makers jumped at the opportunity to use their new found freedom to direct monetary policy toward the laudable objectives of higher real output and employment. Whatever the merits of short-term discretionary monetary changes as far as output and employment are concerned, the experience of the last twenty years makes it clear that in the longer term the prime concern of monetary policy must be with nominal economic variables such as the rate of inflation and the value of total output. The consequence of the collective and simultaneous (if unco-ordinated) actions of governments after Bretton Woods was to inject a major inflationary impulse into the world economic system. Commodity price inflation, which had been relatively dormant since the 1950s, suddenly burst into life. Between 1973 and 1972 commodity prices (excluding oil) rose by 50%. On top of all this, in September 1973, the first oil price shock, the so-called OPEC I took place.

The rest of the decade and the early years of the 1980s were spent trying to deal with the consequences of these events. The period of adjustment was prolonged by the impact of the second oil price shock in 1978, OPEC II. But in broad measure, the consequences were much the same. In absolute terms, the effects of the two oil price shocks on world output and world inflation were not dissimilar. The pendulum was struck with equal force on each occasion and the period from 1973 to 1983 contained two economic cycles of about equal length.

In bald statistical terms, as exemplified in the Tables and Charts, the Age of Prosperity turned into an Age of Instability. The overall behaviour of world inflation is shown in Chart 1, peaking in 1974 and again in 1980. Table 1 looks at the behaviour of real output for selected countries since 1960. The numbers contrast the strong growth of the 1960s with the economic performance of the 1970s and into the 1980s.

To some degree, it was inevitable that the rate of economic growth of the major industrial countries as a whole would slow down as time passed. Much of the growth up to 1970 could be accounted for by the performance of the major European economies and Japan in catching up with the United States, and there is a clear tendency for rates of growth to converge on that of the United States as time has passed. In the 1980s and 1990s, exceptional growth status has passed to the newly industrialising countries. While Japan has reasonably consistently out-performed the other major industrial economies, the disparity in growth rate terms has been much reduced. Interestingly enough, while it is clear that in the majority of cases the potential rate of real output growth fell after 1973, it can be argued that there is little evidence that this is true of the United States.

Chart 1
World Inflation (Consumer prices)

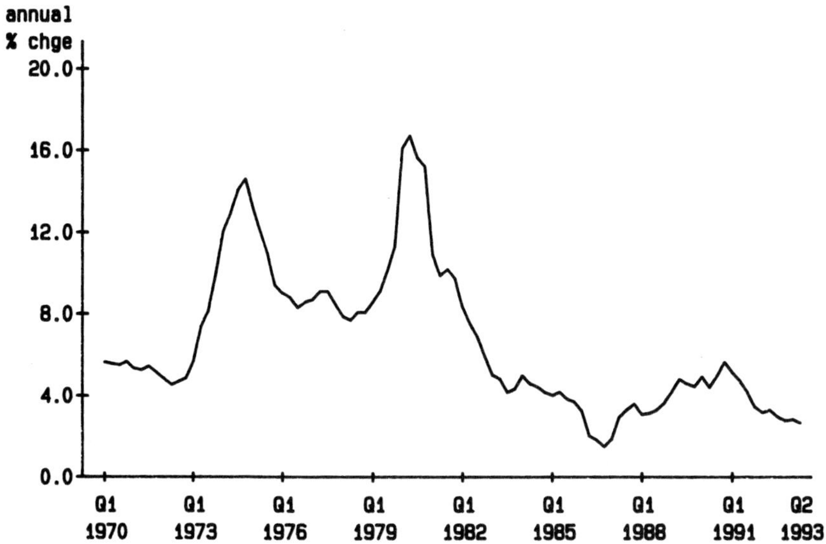

Source: CEF, London Business School, October 1993

Table 1
Economic Growth (GDP)
(average annual % rates of change between the years indicated)

	1960-68	1968-73	1973-79	1979-92
USA	4.5	3.2	2.9	2.1
JAPAN	10.2	8.6	4.2	4.0
GERMANY	4.0	4.9	2.7	2.3
FRANCE	5.4	5.4	3.2	2.2
UK	3.0	3.4	2.3	1.7
CANADA	5.0	4.5	4.7	2.4
EC	4.7	4.9	3.1	2.2
OECD	5.1	4.6	3.3	2.5

Source: Historical Statistics, 1960-90, OECD, Paris OECD Economic Outlook, June 1993

Leaving aside the secular forces affecting the overall rate of growth of world output, there is little doubt of the effect of the oil price shocks in both raising the rate of inflation and generating recession, so lowering the average rate of growth through the 1970s below what it would otherwise have been. A process of learning began which, for some people at least, led to the conclusion that there were no long-run choices or trade-offs between inflation and the behaviour of real output. More than that, inflation was bad for economic growth.

Governmental responses to the crises of the 1970s differed considerably. Some indication of this can be seen by looking at the difference in inflation rates between countries that are set out in Table 2. Initially, as you would expect, given the nature of the Bretton Woods system as already referred to, inflation rates for all the countries are relatively low and bunched together. In the second period, inflation accelerates across the piece, but the bunching remains. But after 1973, both the average rate of inflation and the variance increase sharply. With the notable exception of Germany, the European rate of inflation rises significantly relative to that in both the United States and Japan. Unlike those in US and Japan, European wage levels generally failed to respond to the need to absorb the real costs of the oil price rise. The public sector was favoured at the expense of the private sector, and wages were favoured relative to profits. As a result, relative to North America and Japan, both employment and investment declined. Public sector deficits in Europe grew. The behaviour of the European Community over the period and prior to 1973 can be seen in Table 3. From the European point of view, there began a trend rise in the rate of unemployment that raises a number of questions discussed later in this paper. The general response to the rise in oil prices was to fail to recognise that this was a "real" shock, requiring a cut in real wages relative to labour productivity if the return on capital was not to fall.

Table 2
Consumer Price Inflation

	1960-68	1968-73	1973-79	1979-92
CANADA	2.4	4.6	9.2	5.9
FRANCE	3.6	6.1	10.7	6.4
GERMANY	2.7	4.6	4.7	3.0
JAPAN	5.7	7.1	9.9	2.6
UK	3.6	7.5	15.6	7.1
USA	2.0	5.0	7.6	5.2
EC	3.7	6.1	12.1	7.0
OECD	3.1	5.8	10.3	6.2

Source: Historical Statistics, 1960-90, OECD, Paris OECD Economic Outlook, June 1993

Table 3
Key Indicators of Economic Performance in the Community

	1973/1960	1980/1973	1990/1981	1993[6]/1991
ANNUAL % CHANGE				
Real GDP	4.8	2.2	2.3	1.1
Investment[1]	5.6	0.3	2.5	-0.4
Private consumption deflator	4.6	12.4	6.5	4.7
Unemployment[2,3]	2.3[3]	4.5	9.6	9.6
ANNUAL AVERAGE (% OF GDP)				
Current Account balance	0.5	-0.5	0.2	-0.7
Net borrowing/lending of general government	-0.6[4]	-3.5[5]	-4.4	-5.2

1 Gross fixed capital formation at constant prices.
2 Annual average rate: percentage of civilian labour force.
3 1964-70
4 1970-73 EUR 10: EUR 12 excluding Greece & Portugal.
5 EUR 10: EUR 12 excluding Greece & Portugal.
6 Provisional forecasts, February 1993.

Source: Commission services, European Economy, Annual Economic Report 1993

A significant by-product of the oil price increases was the problem of financing the continual development of third world countries without oil. The so-called recycling problem that developed after 1973 and up to 1978 was handled, apparently successfully, by the world's private banking system. Little of an international cooperative nature appeared to be needed. The IMF put together a modest source of finance, but generally speaking the process of intermediation between third world countries and the oil producers was conducted by banks. However convenient this was for governments, in principle the method of financing was inherently unsatisfactory, mis-matching long term liabilities with short-term assets. In a sense, one might have got away with this after the first round, but the second oil price shock created demands that it was not possible for the banking system to meet without assuming unacceptable risks. In a portfolio sense, the banks were already loaded up to the gills with third world "assets". Moreover, the pressure on capital ratios was intense. This laid the foundation for the so-called debt crisis of the 1980s, which interacted with the problems created by the US fiscal deficit and, at a micro-economic level, cost the banks dear.

As the world began to emerge from the second recession in the early 1980s induced largely by OPEC II, the Reagan administration in the United States embarked on an extraordinary new fiscal strategy.

In over-simplified terms, the administration was persuaded that it could combine major tax reductions aimed at improving the supply side behaviour of the economy with significant increases in government spending on defence, particularly in relation to the Strategic Defence Initiative Programme. Whatever the merits of the tax reduction programme from a supply side point of view, the ultimate effect was a major deterioration in the US fiscal deficit as illustrated in Chart 2. The sequence of events that followed this started with a rise in US interest rates to attract funds, both internally and externally to finance the fiscal deficit. This rise in interest rates encouraged the inflow of external capital which, in the first instance drove up the real exchange rate. The behaviour of the US exchange rate relative to its purchasing power value is illustrated in Chart 3. As the real exchange rate rose, and the competitiveness of the United States declined, the position of the current account also deteriorated. The result of all this was what became subsequently known as the US "twin" deficit problem - the internal fiscal deficit and the external deficit on the current account of the balance of payments.

This created, from 1984 onwards, an overhang on the world economy. The principal problem that affected both politicians and markets throughout the world was how this major disequilibrium in the United States ' financial affairs would be resolved. By the mid-1980s, the scenarios that were being written by many international commentators ranged from a massive recession in the US to correct the balance of payments current account deficiency, to an inflationary debt-reducing outcome with a material fall in the value of the dollar. This issue dominated much of the discussion of the outcome for the world economy during the mid-1980s. When the stock markets of the world fell out of bed in October 1987, many thought that Armageddon had at last come. The world (particularly Japan) would no longer continue to finance the persistent US deficit. It turned out not to be the case. The collapse of Wall Street and London in 1987 was nothing more than a correction to a major short-term financial bubble. Somewhat later in Japan a delayed and far more violent response followed a similar series of events. The combination of the dramatic fall in the oil price in 1986 (OPEC III), combined with the sensible insurance policy taken out by central banks after the 1987 stock market fall, of lower interest rates and increased liquidity in general, conspired to accelerate rates of inflation everywhere. By the end of 1988, the general fear of slump (UK excepted) had turned into a general fear of inflation. World interest rates were rising and the focus of policy-makers was on restoring equilibrium by bringing inflation down.

Chart 2
US Fiscal Deficit
(ratio of government deficit of nominal GDP)

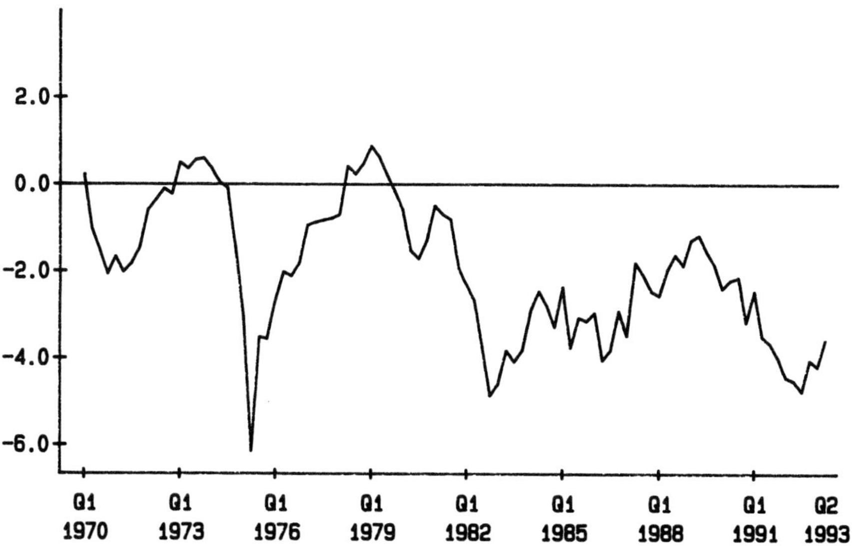

Source: CEF, London Business School, October 1993

In a conjunctural sense that almost brings the story up to date (Summer 1993). The cyclical issue and the policy responses have determined the pattern of economic events over the last six years. The new element that has been of profound importance and which is discussed further below is the re-unification of the German state. This has already (at the time of writing) been significant from a technical economic point of view (e.g. the impact of "high" real German interest rates on the ERM). It also, as will be argued, has profound economic implications for the environment in which Europe in particular will conduct its business in the next decade.

Chart 3
US Dollar
(% deviation from Purchasing Power Parity)

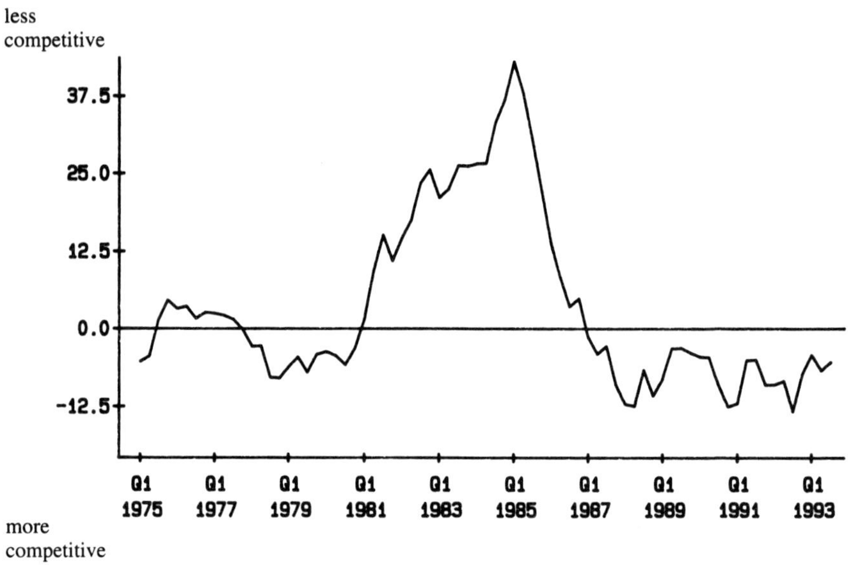

Source: CEF, London Business School, October 1993

This leads us to the economic implications of the end of the Cold War, the last issue of major significance that was referred to earlier. It is always of fundamental importance to remember that economics is political economy. Economic outcomes are directly related to political outcomes, and to the political framework within which the economy operates. While it is difficult to link recent specific economic events to post-Cold War political developments (the case of Germany excepted) as will be argued below, the geo-political changes that have come about have opened up a wider range of possible scenarios for the major players on the international economic scene. But before attempting to discuss these possibilities in any detail, we focus on a number of specific issues that whatever the longer term political outcome are likely to present problems over the next decade.

4. International Trade

As we look forward over the next decade and into the next century it is important to understand the views of our predecessors on important issues such as trade, in order to make some prognosis with regard to future developments. History does repeat itself. But it is important that we do not simply re-invent the wheel. The international economic framework that followed the Bretton Woods Agreement in 1944 was established on the clear assumption that free trade was essential for the prosperity of the post-war world. At the outset it is important to understand why.

Why in 1944 and subsequently was there such a commitment to the idea of free trade? Attitudes to economic issues are affected by the development of ideas, the power exercised by political and business interests, and the ability of existing institutions to shape our destiny. The concern with free trade as a cornerstone of the post-war economic world resulted from a melange of all three forces.

One important factor was undoubtedly the historical judgement that the developments of the 1930s after the crash of 1929 and 1930 were a disaster. One has to bear in mind that developments in the world economy and after the Second World War were dominated by the behaviour of the United States. As will be argued below, American trade policy is still crucial to the health of the economic world as a whole. In response to the recession in the United States, America imposed the most restrictive tariff policy ever seen in the form of the Smoot Hawley tariff of 1930. But by 1934, in the context of a Democratic administration that was emotionally directed toward free trade, protectionist attitudes in the US administration were already on the wane. By 1944, the attitude of the US executive was already pro-free trade. This view was not based on any particular intellectual framework. It was derived simply from the fact that the protectionist philosophy of the early 1930s had failed to deliver what was expected of it.

This conclusion undoubtedly provided the basis for the initial enthusiasm of the United States after the Second World War for free trade. That in itself, however, was not sufficient to sustain US interest in free trade over the next quarter of a century and after. The motivating force for such an interest rested on the belief that free trade and its role in promoting economic prosperity across the world was an essential element in American foreign policy. It was possible for the United States for a long period to run two horses in parallel harness - a belief in the importance of the gains from trade in a free trading world that increased prosperity, and a belief that increasing prosperity under the umbrella of a Pax Americana would provide a solid wall of defence against the encroachment of the Communist world. Good things went together - economic prosperity and a defence of the free market system.

As already described, the financial structure put in place by the Bretton Woods Agreement continued until 1971. Over this period, world trade grew at a rapid pace, consistently faster than the rate of growth of gross national product in the world at large. Some statistics are set out in Table 4. In the sub-periods included in Table 4 it can be seen that the growth in the volume of trade consistently outstripped the growth of gross domestic product by a substantial margin. In Table 5 we can see that the ratio of tradeable goods to non-tradeable goods, reflected in the ratio of export volumes to gross national product, grew substantially.

Table 4
Growth of Output and Trade
average annual % growth

	1960-68	1968-73	1973-79	1979-90
EC				
Output	4.7	4.9	2.5	2.2
Exports	8.4	10.3	5.3	4.1
OECD				
Output	5.1	4.6	2.7	2.7
Exports	8.3	9.7	5.3	4.1

Source: Historical Statistics, 1960-90, OECD, Paris

The exceptional growth rates of the OECD countries prior to the ending of the Bretton Woods exchange rate system in 1971 have already been recorded in Table 1. The important question from the point of view of international trade is to what extent did the liberalisation of trade contribute to the extraordinary period of growth and prosperity after the Second World War? As already seen, trade in the OECD countries grew substantially faster in real terms than gross domestic product. It is clear that the rapid underlying growth of real output in the OECD was affected by circumstances other than the liberalisation of trade. Industrial countries outside the United States, including particularly the defeated countries, Germany and Japan, had the great opportunity to catch up with the United States. Cheap energy and cheap raw materials encouraged profitable growth in the manufacturing countries of the OECD. Financial stability was a necessary, if not a sufficient, condition for this age of growth and prosperity. But even after allowing for these factors, it is difficult to believe on *prima facie* grounds that the liberalisation of trade over this period was not of crucial importance.

Table 5
Exports of Goods & Services as % of GDP

	1960-67	1968-73	1974-79	1980-90
USA	5.2	5.8	8.4	8.5
Japan	9.8	10.6	12.6	12.7
Germany	18.5	21.2	25.4	29.9
France	13.3	15.6	20.2	22.3
UK	19.9	22.6	28.2	26.2
Canada	18.8	22.2	24.5	26.9
EC	18.8	21.3	25.7	28.2
OECD	12.4	14.0	17.3	18.4

Source: Historical Statistics, 1960-90, OECD, Paris

The new institutions of the post-war economic world were intended to reflect the principal issues of concern. The International Monetary Fund was created to act as a cyclical lender of funds to smooth out the short-term balance of payments problems of individual countries over the trade cycle within a pegged exchange rate framework. The International Bank for Reconstruction and Development (World Bank) was to serve as the principal financial intermediator between the rich and poor countries with regard to economic development. A further organization, the International Trade Organization, was to serve as the major organization dealing not just with trade but also with restrictive business practices and international commodity agreements. The power of the United States at the time is illustrated by the fact that it was Congress that threw it out. What was left was the chapter on trade that gave rise to the General Agreement on Tariffs and Trade that produced the subsequent framework for the reduction of trade barriers between nations.

The three essential principles of the GATT were reciprocity, the mutual recognition of change, non-discrimination, meaning a concession granted to one was granted to all, and transparency, the recognition of discrimination in terms of tariffs rather than non-tariff barriers. The tactical procedures of the GATT, and the implementation of the GATT principles, were contained in a series of "rounds" of negotiations since the Second World War, leading up to the current round of negotiations in the so-called Uruguay Round. The effect of the negotiations in these rounds on tariffs is illustrated in Chart 4, which looks at the succession of tariff negotiating rounds and their effect on tariffs in the United States. It can be seen from Chart 4, the pattern of which can be widely extended elsewhere, that the GATT rounds were very successful in reducing the general level of tariff barriers in the OECD. At the same time, specific tariff reductions within individual areas, notably the European Community, were also encouraging the growth of trade.

Chart 4

Index (Pre-Geneva Average Tariff = 100)

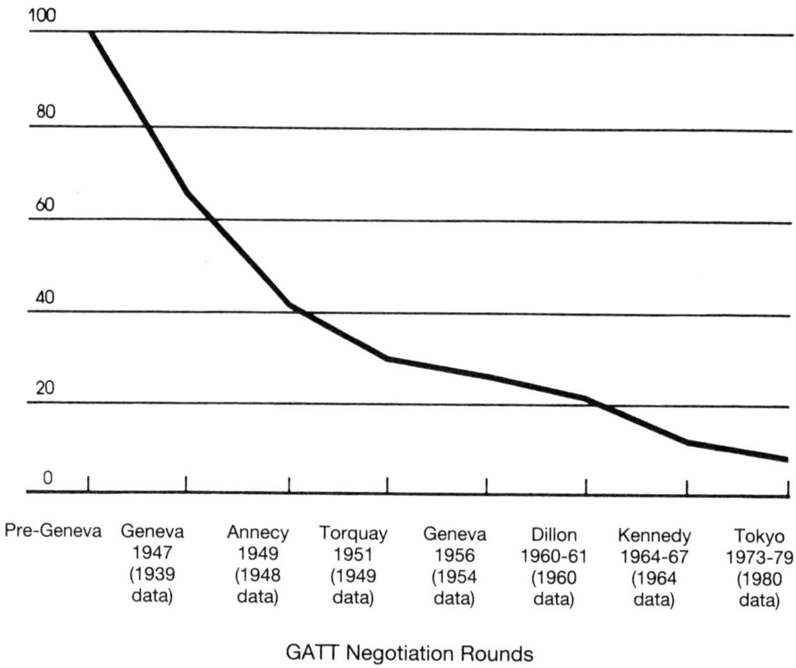

Figure 1 Reductions in average U.S. tariff rates after GATT rounds. Indexes are calculated from percentage reductions in average weighted tariff rates given in Finger 1979 (table 1, page 425) and World Bank 1987 (table 8.1, page 136). Weighted average U.S. tariff rate after Tokyo Round was 4.6 percent (World Bank 1987).

To summarise, the growth of trade after the Second World War was a major contributor to the economic growth of the OECD countries. It was strongly supported by the United States, which saw it in part as an antidote to the economic failure of the 1930s, and in part as an essential ingredient in American foreign and security policy. The economic strength of the United States enabled it to take a liberal view toward trade policies when combined with national foreign policy and security benefits, despite the palpable existence of free riders on such a policy. Against this background, the United States turned a blind eye to restrictive trade practices in Japan, encouraged the development of the European Economic Community, and opened US markets to others. It supported the development of GATT and the extension of multilateral trade in general on GATT principles.

As already recorded, at the beginning of the BNAC in 1969, Harry Johnson believed that in large measure much had been achieved by the GATT. True, there remained a serious problem with regard to agriculture, and no attempt had been made to bring services into consideration. But for trade in goods outside these categories, liberalisation from his point of view had been substantially realised and there were few signs on the horizon of the potential difficulties that were to come in the following two decades.

As matters stand today, at no time since the Second World War has the principle of free trade been under such threat. In Johnson's time, the free trade principle was so self-evident that it did not warrant detailed discussion. Of course, free trade was seen to bring its problems of adjustment but in that age of expansion and optimism nothing seemed insurmountable. There is little doubt, however, that the widespread use of non-tariff as opposed to tariff barriers to trade have to some extent offset the tariff reductions carried on through the successive GATT rounds. In the United States itself, there have been strident calls to abandon the universal principle of free trade in return for some concept of "managed trade". To forecast the future, it is necessary to understand why this has taken place.[3]

There are principally four reasons why attitudes to trade have changed, which have contributed to the difficulties that have surrounded the Uruguay Trade Round.

The first is derived from the macro-economic instability that followed the collapse of the Bretton Woods exchange rate arrangements and the oil price shocks of the 1970s. As was the case in the 1930s, the wide fluctuations in

---

[3] See my earlier paper "The Causes of Rising Protectionism", *BNARA Occasional Paper 7*, November 1987

both nominal and real exchange rates over the last twenty years have provided ammunition for those supporting more general demands for protection and for managed trade. An excellent example is provided by the American experience of the 1980s in which a major decline in US competitiveness (as seen earlier in Chart 2) resulted from the consequences of the US fiscal deficit for US interest rates and, therefore, the dollar. The resulting deterioration in the US current account of the balance of payments is largely attributable to fiscal imbalance rather than a loss of structural competitiveness. The recessions of the mid-1970s, the early 1980s and the late 1980s/early 1990s, all served to re-focus the self-interest of individual economies away from collective concerns. Recession raises the question of survival for particular industries. Adjustments to trading patterns, easy to accommodate on the back of a steady rise in prosperity, become individual disasters in a rollercoaster world.

The second factor that has focussed on managed trade has been the rise in the economic importance of Japan and the Asian Tigers. While the point has been debated (e.g. with regard to the steel industry) there is a major presumption that with respect to large parts of its traditional high volume manufacturing activities in technologically based products, textiles, a wide range of metal and engineering activities, and shipping, the West has become inherently uncompetitive. Whether true or not, the belief has been there.

Thirdly, antagonism toward free trade outside the European Union (and particularly in North America) has been generated by suspicion about the objectives of the Union itself. On the face of it, the Union's progress toward the so-called Single Market has been based on a belief in the free trade principle as a means of encouraging internal prosperity. But many outside the Union have raised the fear of Fortress Europe - a plot to close off access for those outside the Union to its supposedly new and expanding market, a fear that imputes a coherence to the European Union which it does not have. To potential insult has been added perceived injury in the form of the Common Agricultural Policy and its implications for world trade in agricultural products, an issue that has assumed excessive importance in the negotiations in the Uruguay Round.

Finally, there is little doubt that the attitude of the United States has been influenced by its own perception of its relative decline in terms of economic importance. As can be seen in Table 6, the share of the United States in world real gross domestic product has declined substantially over the last 40 years.

This perception of relative decline, coupled with the ending of the Cold War, and the shift in the world position on security means that the United

States no longer retains the same motivation towards free trade that characterised the first quarter century after the Second World War. A combination of events, the rise of Asia, the development of the European Union and the end of the Cold War have all in different ways undermined the political case for free trade in North America generally. At the same time, as explained in a forthcoming BNAC publication, in parallel there has been an attempt to undermine its intellectual basis.[4]

The classical theory of the gains from trade was stated simply by Ricardo over a century and a half ago. It was based on a simple model of perfect competition and diminishing returns to scale, and explained how, through the principle of comparative advantage, specialisation of production and exchange between countries would lead to higher levels of output and collectively greater welfare. The conclusions that could be derived from this simple model were powerful indeed - they reflected the proposition that free trade between nations was a universal good.

Table 6
Allocation of World Gross Domestic Product (1990)
% of World Output*

	1965	1990	
OECD	68.2	71.7	
Rest of the World	31.8	28.3	
European Community	22.7	26.9	
United States	34.3	24.1	
Japan	4.47	13.1	
European Community as % of OECD	33.3	37.4	
United States as % of OECD	50.3	33.7	89.5% of OECD
Japan as % of OECD	6.6	18.7	

Source: World Development Report 1992, World Bank,
Table 3: Structure of Production
**excluding former USSR & North Korea*

The starting point of the "new" theory of international trade is to observe that the world is not dominated by perfectly competitive conditions - it is

[4] See R Belous and F M Scherer, ""Unfinished Tasks: New International Trade Theory & the Post-Uruguay Challenge," *BNAC Issues Paper*, No 3, May 1993.

indeed very imperfect with a strong tendency toward oligopolies in manufacturing industry in particular. Moreover, it is also clear that increasing returns to scale are more likely to be the rule rather than the exception and that learning curves play an important role in improving efficiency. Having established these facts (correctly) the next stage of the argument is to borrow recent developments from the theory of industrial economics which have applied ideas from game theory to the competitive strategic moves by firms. This leads to the idea of what has been called Strategic Trade Theory which substitutes countries for firms in the analysis and envisages the emergence of new potential gains or "rents" for individual countries by playing "games" through the use of taxes, subsidies and other devices in international trade.

It is certainly true that once imperfect competition and economies of scale are allowed for it is no longer possible to prove the general propositions that Ricardo advanced. However, empirical studies have demonstrated, on a case by case basis, that the gains from trade given such an environment are often much greater than the traditional theory would lead you to expect. On an intuitive basis, this is because the development of trade over the last thirty years has substantially reflected the growth of *intra-trade* as contrasted with *inter-trade*, the subject that Ricardo dealt with. Inter-trade is simply trade in unlike things, wine for shirts for example, while intra-trade exchanges like for like, cars with cars and machine tools with machine tools. Additional welfare can therefore be generated by niche market specialists and greater variety supported by branding. Benefits may be created through trade therefore in addition to those produced by a re-allocation of productive resources amongst existing uses.

The central point of the new Strategic Trade Theory can probably be expressed by saying that comparative advantage in trade does not fall as the gentle rain from heaven but can be created. The question then arises as to what policies need to be followed by governments in order to sustain competitiveness. Here the views divide. Some believe that the new Strategic Trade Theory provides an agenda for government actions. Others sceptically regard the process as providing the old Emperor with a set of new clothes to justify the ways in which governments have been trying to behave in times past.

Finally, it is possible to link attitudes to free trade, particularly with regard to industrial goods, with the concern in many quarters about the process of de-industrialisation. The major increase in non-tariff barriers to trade, and a main focus of many of the calls for managed trade, has been in manufactures. In the Anglo-Saxon world, there has been a concern that not only has manufacturing industry some unique role to play in the process of economic growth, it has in addition a special significance for the current account of the balance of payments. This issue also relates to the question of employment - where are the jobs coming from? - which is discussed later in this paper.

The difficulties of completing the Uruguay Round have not resulted simply from the combined effects of the factors that have been described which have influenced attitudes to free trade. It can be argued that problems stemmed initially from the tactical approach of the United States in demanding the total abolition of agricultural subsidies and price support programmes. It was unrealistic to believe that the Europeans would ever have gone as far as the United States was asking. Moreover, even with the United States, it was doubtful whether the implementation of such a programme was politically feasible in the farming states.

The Uruguay Round, starting in Punte de Este in September 1986 reflected the most complex negotiating problems yet seen. As well as dealing with traditional problems of market access, it extended to agriculture, textiles, services, intellectual property and inward investment. To over-simplify it, the wealthier countries were to open their markets for manufactures and agricultural products, while the developing countries were to guarantee intellectual property rights and open themselves to overseas investment and financial services.

The agreement finally cobbled together in December 1993 had all the hallmarks of an expected compromise (the exclusion of certain media issues for example). But nevertheless, it represents a significant step forward. At the worst, it can be seen to represent an unwillingness to take a significant step backwards.

The achievement of open trading relations cannot be assessed in terms of a simple economic calculation. The first and obvious reason is that it is technically extremely difficult to do so. Numbers such as “an addition of $200 bn to world trade by the year 2000” are incredibly difficult to validate. Most analyses are static rather than dynamic, like the way in which the Economic Union tried to calculate the economic benefits of the Single European Market. The dynamic effects, which may turn out to be major, are scarcely predictable. There is an act of faith.

But, secondly, open trade relations are an essential element in the character of political relations in general. Nations that relate to each other from behind economic protective walls often brew dangerous political potions. The American instinct, that after the Second World War free trade was a key factor in inspiring stable political associations in the West, was a wise one.

The alternative to multinational trade is to see the world divide itself into trading blocs. From a theoretical point of view, such blocs may introduce major inefficiencies into the use of economic resources, since such arrangements do not only create trade, they also divert it. But there may be little harm in the development of particularly close relations between trading groups such as the European Union, and more recently the new North American Free Trade Area, provided that these developments are seen within the framework of a more global trading system.

However, even given recent agreement with regard to both NAFTA and the GATT, these developments must be seen only as steps clearing the way to a more coherent multilateral system. The debates will continue. There still remains much scepticism about the universal principle of free trade and the future role of GATT. We cannot be so confident about the future of world trade as was Harry Johnson two decades ago. The impetus for free trade after the Second World War came largely from the United States, for the reasons already presented, neither of which currently have any force. Harry Johnson foresaw the need for major changes in the system of agricultural protection and that need remains in place today. On that issue, in the light of European attitudes, it is difficult to do other than echo Johnson's scepticism. Further progress in the liberalisation of, and orderly conduct of trade in services will have to wait.

Those who believe that governments, through the applications of strategic trade policies, can create welfare for their countries will no doubt have more optimism for the future than those who believe that the liberalisation of trade in general is a major benefit for the world at large. For them, there are perhaps three rays of hope.

The first is that despite the gloomy tone of much of what has gone before, the fact of the matter is that as can be seen from Table 4 trade has continued to grow faster than real output. This is sometimes explained by an argument that runs as follows. Basically it says governments as such tend to be more free trade oriented than the forces that besiege them. The barriers they introduce, it is said, in order to appease the lobbies, tend to be "porous" i.e. possible to get through in some degree. Therefore, the impact of such measures is less than you would expect.

Secondly, there is an argument that says that the world is now too interdependent for industrial countries to cut off their trading links in ways in which they were able to do in times past. The increasing globalisation of the world economy and the importance not only of trade but also direct investment will make it increasingly difficult to step too far back from the current position in which we find ourselves.

Thirdly, while the industrialised countries in the West debate the issue of managed trade, the developing countries and the countries of Eastern Europe are realising what a disaster the pursuit of various forms of managed trade have been for their economic health. In the developing counties, the opening up of domestic markets to both goods and capital offers a basis for transformation that will be of benefit not only to individual economies but also to the world at large.

The bottom line is probably that, while progress toward a correction of the anomalies in agriculture protection and free trade in services will be slow, the recent GATT agreement suggests that the steps backward may not be as bad as some fear. Trade will probably be sustained by an increase in the opening of trade on a regional, if not a fully multilateral basis. Whatever the outcome of current developments in the European Union, a retreat into intra-European protectionism in the immediate future is unlikely. Trade is likely to develop in part within the framework of trading groupings such as the Union and North America. Developments in the Asia Pacific Region will be complicated by the rise of China to be a major trading power by the end of the century. This will pose increasing problems for Japan in avoiding isolation in the region, given the likely increased links between China and the diaspora Chinese.

5. Inflation and the International Monetary System

The golden age of growth and prosperity that followed the Second World War was, as we have seen accompanied by financial stability in the trading world in terms of stable exchange rates and by the standards of what came later, low inflation. As remarked earlier, while financial stability may not be a sufficient condition for economic growth, it is certainly necessary.

An efficient financial system within which international trade takes place should ideally contribute to three objectives. The first is the provision of a framework that encourages and facilitates trading relationships. Secondly, the system should be such as to make it relatively easy to absorb real macro-economic shocks that occur in the trading world. Thirdly, the system should provide a mechanism that enables financial stability to be maintained - what this boils down to in practice is controlling the overall rate of world inflation.

As we have seen, as a result of the Bretton Woods Agreement, these objectives were substantively achieved for a quarter of a century after the War. That achievement depended essentially on the economic position of the United States and the way it conducted its monetary and fiscal policy before the Vietnam war developed. The ending of the commitment of the major countries to tie their currencies to the dollar was followed by the adoption of floating exchange rates (leaving on one side the attempts of the European Community members to stabilise currency movements within Europe). The financial history of the post-Bretton Woods era may be captured by the history of nominal exchange rates, interest rates and the real supply of money in Charts 5, 6 and 7. All these financial indicators exhibit substantial fluctuations over the 1970s and the 1980s, leading, as we have seen, to pressure on trading relationships and protectionism.

The move to floating rates that was widely accepted in the 1970s resulted in a loss of interest in the discussions about and proposals for reforming the international monetary system at large. Members of the then Economic Community put exchange rate stability high on the agenda of the Community and established the ERM in 1979 (without the United Kingdom!). But it was not until 1985 that the US Administration, in the shape of James Baker, as Secretary to the Treasury, began to take the view that exchange rate stability might be of major importance. The behaviour of the dollar both as effect and cause of the US twin deficit problem at last rang some alarm bells in Washington and encouraged the discussion of exchange rates at the series of summits that have taken place since.

Chart 5
Nominal Exchange Rates against the Dollar

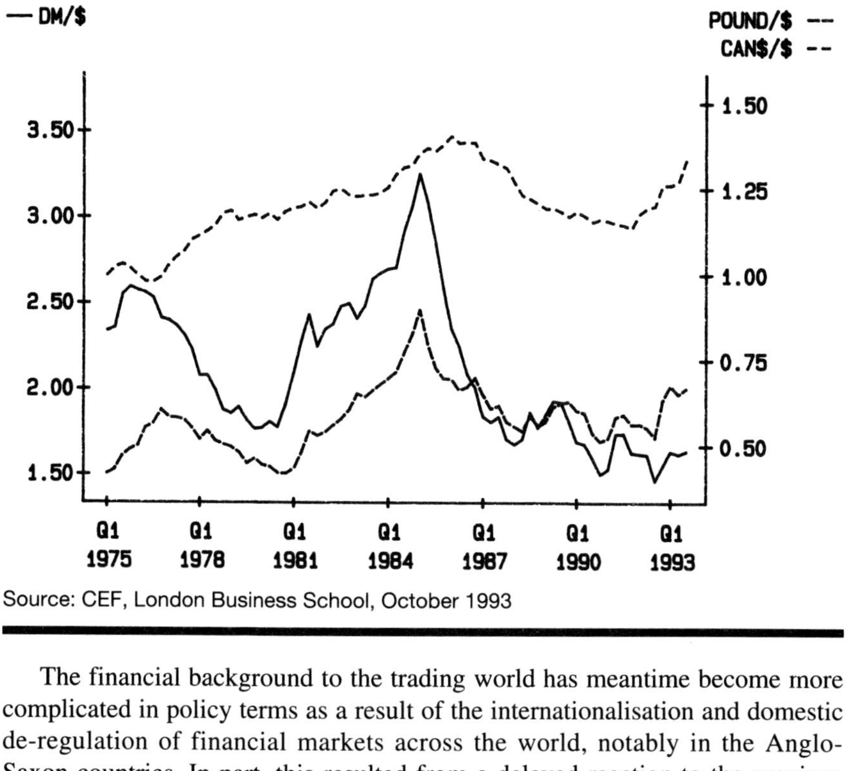

Source: CEF, London Business School, October 1993

The financial background to the trading world has meantime become more complicated in policy terms as a result of the internationalisation and domestic de-regulation of financial markets across the world, notably in the Anglo-Saxon countries. In part, this resulted from a delayed reaction to the previous period of trade liberalisation, in part from changes in attitudes to market behaviour, and in part because of developments in technology, that, from a financial point of view at least, encouraged the idea of the global village. The earliest manifestation of some of the problems that the globalisation of finance might bring could be seen in the development of the Euro-dollar market in the 1960s and even more in the 1970s. Global financial integration has posed new problems for both economic policy makers and regulators in individual countries.

Chart 6
Interest Rates (3-month rates)

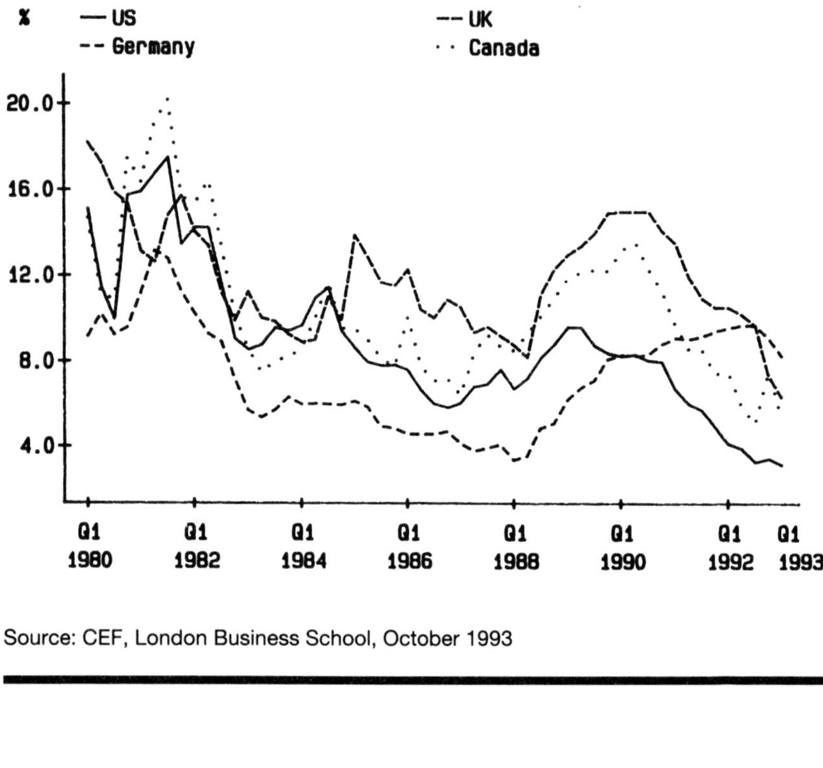

Source: CEF, London Business School, October 1993

Having said that, it should not be thought that such developments have created insoluble problems or that financial liberalisation has not brought great benefits. Financial liberalisation on a world scale results in major potential gains with regard to the efficient allocation of capital resources that should emerge from the equalisation of rates of return and real resource transfers. The major benefit has probably been to improve capital market efficiency in general. Niche market specialisation on a world scale (the financial analogue of "intra-trade"), the ability to diversify, the opening up of financial markets and economies of scale in intermediation all should in principle contribute to a reduction in the real cost of capital. As a starting point for discussion of the future of the international monetary system it is not easy to see that the developments of the 1970s and 1980s will be easily reversed.

Chart 7
Real World Money Supply
(for G7 countries)

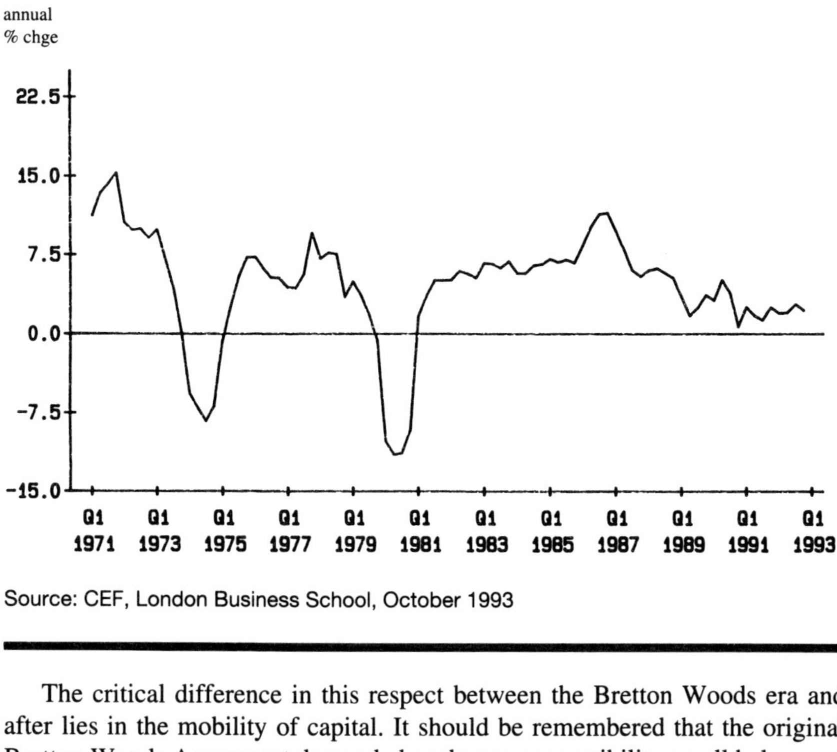

Source: CEF, London Business School, October 1993

The critical difference in this respect between the Bretton Woods era and after lies in the mobility of capital. It should be remembered that the original Bretton Woods Agreement demanded exchange convertibility on all balance of payments current account transactions. However, discrimination against capital movements was positively encouraged. This arose from the belief that capital movements in the 1930s had been destabilising - movements of so-called "hot money" from centre to centre had been responsible for the instability of interest rates and exchange rates during that period. This suspicion of and restraint of capital movements after the war was partly responsible for the excessive concentration on current account behaviour of the balance of payments for individual countries. In the absence of a return to the widespread use again of exchange rate controls on capital movements, the benefits from and the problems raised by capital mobility will continue to be with us for the rest of the decade.

Economic theory tells us that other things being equal, in the long run, exchange rates will reflect the relative behaviour of nominal prices - the so-called purchasing power parity theory of exchange rates. The history of the last twenty years has demonstrated that exchange rates can move significantly away from their purchasing power parities, and such divergence can persist for material periods of time. Chart 3 that illustrates the behaviour of the dollar makes the point. Despite this, there is a strong case for believing that in the longer run nominal exchange rate behaviour is substantively affected by inflation rates. Putting it another way, it is difficult to envisage wild fluctuations in nominal exchange rates in a world of stable prices. This suggests that it is the control of the inflation rate that is crucial to international financial stability in general.

It has been argued above that after 1971 countries realised that with the end of the Bretton Woods exchange rate agreement they had regained control of their own monetary policy, and that this meant in practice a major responsibility for their own inflation rate. This is of course not strictly true, except in a world of perfectly floating exchange rates. Even with floating rates it is difficult if not impossible for individual economies to entirely avoid the knock-on consequences of a major boost to world inflation, although as illustrated by West Germany in the 1970s, the impact may be substantially mitigated. It took some time, however, for economists, civil servants, and politicians to accept (as had been clear to the late Harry Johnson) that fluctuations in inflation rates are primarily associated with fluctuations in the supply of money. Nevertheless, despite what now may seem obvious to many of us, debates on the subject continue both within and without the academic profession. Whatever the disagreements about the precise mechanism that determines changes in inflation rates, recent debate has focussed on an even more fundamental issue, namely the extent to which inflation actually matters. The conclusion of this debate has clearly profound significance for the attitude of policy-makers in the foreseeable future. As matters stand, there is no doubt that the control of inflation in the three countries represented in the BNAC has, during the 1980s been elevated to a leading position on the agenda of central banks and governments alike. The questions that this poses currently are two-fold. Firstly, what are the social costs of inflation that justify such an attitude? Secondly, does this mean that we can expect a lower inflation environment in the foreseeable future than we have been exposed to over the last twenty years?

Attitudes to inflation in the major industrial countries in the 1960s and early 1970s (with the notable exception of Germany) reflected the view that there was a permanent trade-off between unemployment and the inflation rate. The cost of maintaining full employment might turn out to be a higher rate of inflation than was thought desirable. At best, full employment and economic growth could be bought by accepting higher inflation that would otherwise be the case. The experience of the 1970s and the early 1980s, however, suggested that not only had the short-term trade-off between unemployment and inflation in the OECD become less advantageous, in the longer run no permanent trade-off existed. But this conclusion remains contentious, and some question what they see as a sacrifice in both employment and economic growth in order to sustain a low inflation rate. There is no dispute as to the fact that there are real costs incurred in the process of reducing the inflation rate from a "high" to a "low" level.

The costs of a fully anticipated and stable inflation rate are familiar - the cost of economising on real money balances (the "shoe-leather" effect), the cost of recording price changes (the "menu costs"), the costs of indexation (particularly of the tax system) and front- loading of the real burden of servicing nominal debt contracts. But of course a world of fully anticipated stable inflation is totally unrealistic. These costs have usually seemed acceptable to the "expansionists". Inflation in practice has not been stable, and, therefore, has certainly been very imperfectly anticipated.

The additional costs of unanticipated inflation are equally familiar, even if there are disagreements about how important they are. The first is that it makes it difficult for economic agents in goods and financial markets to distinguish between changes in absolute and changes in relative prices. This confuses the free market process of generating an efficient allocation of resources which depends essentially on relative prices alone. The signalling system is distorted. This process is most important in distinguishing between nominal and real rates of interest. When inflation is not anticipated, investors and savers cannot know the real rate of interest or rates of return with any degree of certainty, which makes for inappropriate investment decisions. Secondly, there is a major loss of output and welfare that results from the impact on the distribution of income and wealth particularly between debtors and creditors. Like theft, inflation is just the redistribution of income without parliamentary approval. Moreover, high nominal interest rates encourage short-termism in investment decisions, and inflation tends to raise the cost of capital by an additional risk premium. Thirdly, it encourages major activity in terms of arrangements, risk management and tax evasion designed to protect people from its consequences.

Despite these undoubtedly important considerations there are still those who believe that the control of inflation is a matter of secondary importance. The general thesis is that there is a permanent resource cost in controlling inflation - i.e. it is not simply a monetary phenomenon. Some who hold this view also recognise that there are costs that arise from inflation itself, and tend therefore to a popular view that there is a reasonable limit (perhaps 5%?) below which the costs of reducing the inflation rate exceed the benefits. Sometimes this is put by saying that a "little" inflation is a good thing that will oil the growth mechanism and keep the wheels of industry turning.

This seductive point of view is unfortunately not a serious option (even if it would have the desired effect). Alcoholism is rarely cured by moderate drinking. Unless there is a total commitment to abstinence, the cure will be ineffective. However, it should be clear that in the case of inflation, this does not necessarily mean an objective of zero inflation. The issue has been well articulated by Alan Greenspan.

> "For all practical purposes, price stability means that expected changes in the average price level are small enough and gradual enough that they do not materially enter business and household decisions."[5]

The number that seems to have surfaced in a number of countries that is seen as consistent with this definition is of the order of 2% - perhaps the amount that the official statisticians tend to overestimate the inflation rate through a failure to adjust for quality changes.

Against this background, what is the prognosis? There are a number of points to take into consideration. In the first place, as can be seen from the United Kingdom illustration in Chart 8, taking the long view of history (as we can approximate it) inflation has been the exception rather than the norm. It is possible to take the view that from a world point of view, the inflationary experience of the 1970s and the early 1980s represents an unusual period marked by the effects of oil price increases, the collapse of Bretton Woods and the specific responses of individual governments, particularly with regard to monetary policy. Hopefully, something has been learned from that experience with regard to the significance of monetary policy and its effects on inflation rates.

---

[5] A Greenspan, *Federal Reserve Bulletin*, April 1989, Washington (report of a speech given to the US Senate Committee on Banking, Housing and Urban Affairs on 21 February 1989)

Insofar as monetary policy, and in particularly monetary growth, is accepted as the key to the inflationary economy, at least in the medium term, the question arises as to why should we anticipate a major monetary expansion on a world scale in the foreseeable future? Of course there may well be shocks that we cannot reasonably anticipate. But probably the most likely driver of loose monetary policies remains the danger of loose fiscal policies and the tendency of politicians to monetise the national debt. The extent to which they are likely to do so depends in large measure on whether as discussed above the electors have fully taken on board what the costs of inflation really are. These pressures are further discussed in relation to expanding public expenditure below.

Chart 8

The United Kingdom Price Level 1270-1991

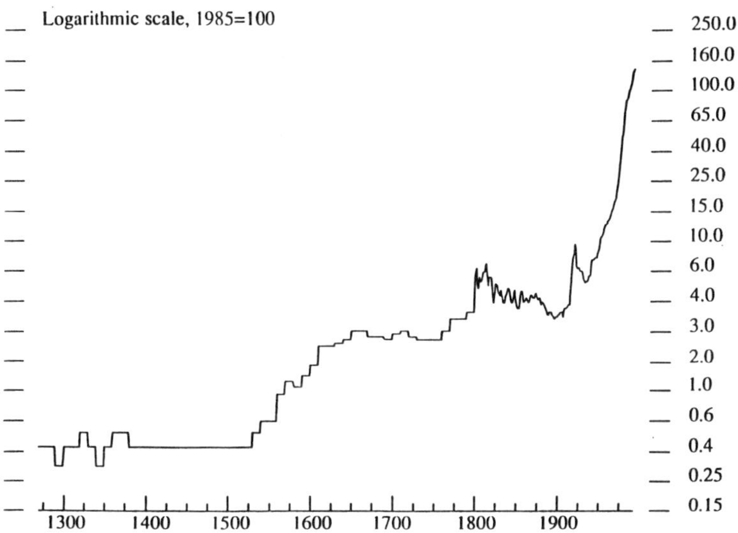

Source: Bank of England

Source: Copy of speech given by Rt Hon Robin Leigh Pemberton, Governor of the Bank of England at LSE, No 11, 1992

However, in the shorter run, there are two further factors that may be taken into account. The first is the generally downward price pressure in the OECD countries at least that is emanating from competition and the suggested declining importance of branded products. The inability of major international companies to exact premium price increases in world markets has been affecting stock market evaluations across the world. Secondly, there is little doubt that across the OECD, there has been a significant decline in the power of organised labour that has weakened the power of the so-called price/wage cost inflation mechanism, which, with continuing relatively high unemployment rates in the foreseeable future, is unlikely to strengthen. These micro-economic pressures are likely to remain with us for the rest of the century.

All this suggests that the odds are in favour of inflation returning to the sort of rates that we were used to experiencing in the 1950s and the 1960s - there is no reason to invoke the spectre of deflation and falling prices that characterised the 1930s. The upward pressure on public spending should see to that! But even inflation of this kind will have implications for business, a need to keep costs strictly under control, and for investors with a need to focus even more closely on real returns. In a low inflation world, debts are real and must be paid back in real money. Firms, householders and pension funds can no longer be bailed out by massive doses of inflation.

However, as already emphasised, inflation is not simply a domestic matter except in some artificially pure regime of floating exchange rates. The future course of inflation will also depend on the way in which the international monetary system functions, a subject to which we now turn.

As we have seen, concern about the reform of the international monetary system disappeared in the early seventies to re-appear in the mid-eighties. Debates about the subject polarise around two views about the behaviour of and importance of exchange rates.

The first argues essentially that there is nothing much wrong with the international monetary system as such. The principal concern of those who see the need for international monetary reform usually rest their case on the erratic behaviour and unpredictability of nominal exchange rates. But, the argument goes, the fact that exchange rates are hard to predict is an obvious characteristic of an efficient market. Just because you find stock prices difficult to predict doesn't call for a wholesale reform of the stock market. Why exchange rates fluctuate, so the argument goes, is not a consequence of the system but is simply the consequence of the behaviour of the macro-economic policies that individual countries pursue. Putting the matter another way, the central issue is not to make a choice between a system of managed floating and some other system of pegged rates, since if governments already have the will to follow appropriate macro-policies exchange rates will stabilise.[6]

The alternative view can be characterised as coming at the problem from the opposite direction. Whereas those in favour of managed floating emphasise the effect of policy on exchange rates, those in favour of pegged exchange rates emphasise the effect of the exchange rate objective on policy itself. Oversimplifying, it boils down to whether you have more optimism about a system (pegged rates) that is designed to reduce short term policy discretion rather than a system that leaves sovereignty and full discretion in the hands of domestic policy makers (managed floating). Ultimately it is not a question of economic theory, but a question of the way in which policy makers behave. For example, some believe that the way in which politicians behave under floating rates has been shown historically to be inherently inflationary - hence the calls for central banks to be independent of governments.

The universal collapse of the ERM at the time of writing must be seen as a set-back to the hopes of those who saw the ERM model as a step toward not simply a single European currency but also a more general framework of pegged rates. Over the next decade the issue of international monetary stability will remain a critical one for the international trading world. But that stability will continue to rest on the efforts of the individual players rather than any significant increase in international co-operation. There has been much discussion of a possible way forward in terms of the establishment of 'target zones' for the G7 countries for economic variables such as interest rate and inflation rates. But since these ideas surfaced a decade ago there has been no progress in translating them into practice.

---

[6]These arguments are well set out in J A Frenkel "The International Monetary System; Should it be Reformed?", *American Economic Review,* May 1987

6. Employment

Following the disastrous experience of the thirties, unemployment rates in the OECD countries fell to relatively low levels after the Second World War and remained there until the late sixties. A gradual increase thereafter became a sharp increase in many countries after the rise in oil prices in 1973. The average rates of unemployment continued to deteriorate into the eighties as can be seen in Table 7. The increase in unemployment rates was most marked in the countries of the European Union, but it is worth noting that such an increase did not take place in the so-called EFTA countries (which include Norway, Sweden, Finland, Austria and Switzerland). Unemployment also trended up in the United States, although less markedly, while the specific nature of employment in Japan probably made it somewhat *sui generis*. What is clear is that while there has been general pressure at work that has affected unemployment rates in general in the OECD, there have been wide differences in rates between individual countries.

Table 7
Unemployment Rates 1960-1990

	1960-68	1969-73	1974-79	1980-85	1986-90
OECD[1]	2.2	2.4	4.2	7.2	7.3
EC[2]	2.4	2.8	5.2	10.1	10.4
EFTA[3]	1.4	1.4	2.0	3.0	3.0

1 OECD 19 countries
2 EC 9 countries
3 EFTA 5 countries

Source: Layard, Nickell & Jackman, *Unemployment,* 1991

It has been argued that if unemployment is looked at over very long periods there is no pronounced trend. Data for the UK and the USA (such as they are) going back to the 19th century are shown in Charts 9 and 10. The lack of trend over the period, it is suggested, shows that ultimately there are very powerful mechanisms at work which have forced the number of jobs to respond to huge changes that have occurred in the numbers of people wanting work. It is also concluded that the absence of any very long term trend implies that in the long run the unemployment rate is independent of the level of productivity - which can be interpreted as saying that in the long run technological unemployment is unlikely.[7]

Unemployment since the Nineteenth Century
Chart 9 (a) UK

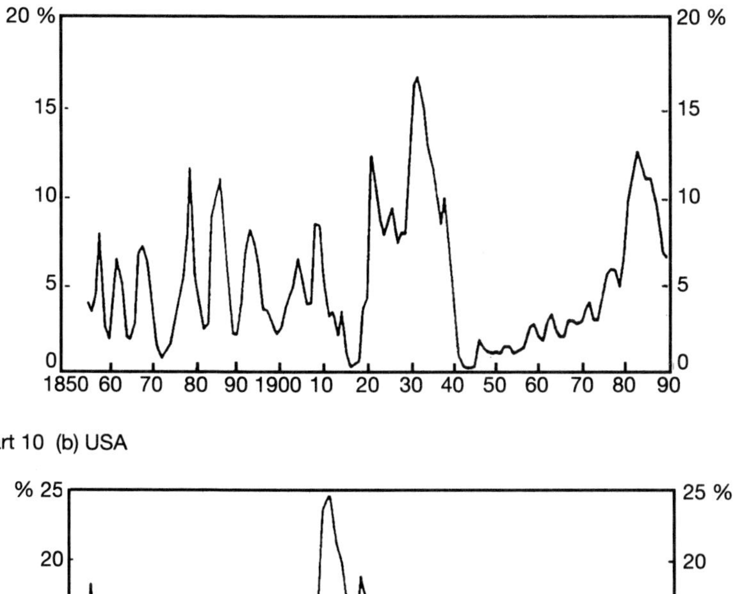

Chart 10 (b) USA

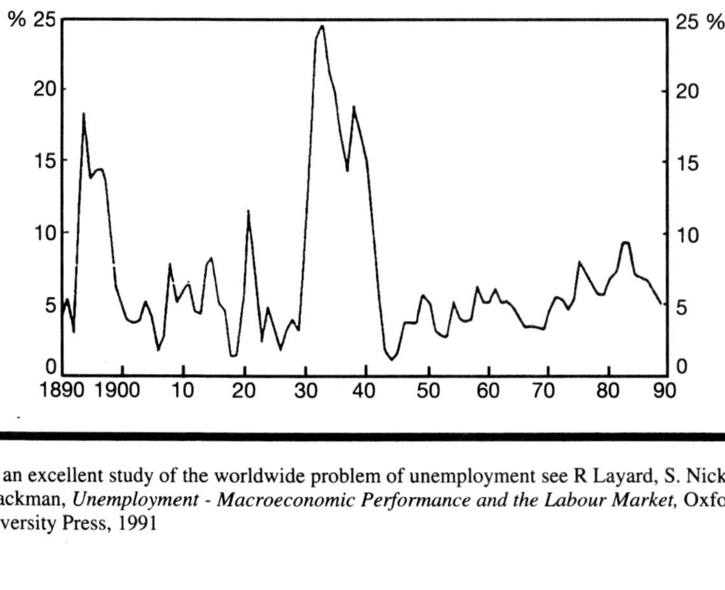

[7] For an excellent study of the worldwide problem of unemployment see R Layard, S. Nickell and R Jackman, *Unemployment - Macroeconomic Performance and the Labour Market,* Oxford University Press, 1991

Who are the unemployed? Clearly there are significant differences in unemployment rates between age groups, occupations, region, races and genders. Moreover these differences also vary between countries. Generally speaking young people are much more likely to be unemployed than older people, and this has led policy makers in many countries to regard unemployment as essentially a young people's problem. However the evidence suggests that the most important factor affecting differences in unemployment rates is occupation. It has been estimated that unemployment rates for semi- and unskilled workers are four to five times higher than for professional and managerial workers. From this it has been concluded that the principal focus of the study of unemployment should be the labour market for manual workers.

Illustrative data for the UK and USA are given in Table 8. Table 8 breaks down the inflow rate into the stock of unemployment, the average duration of unemployment and the actual unemployment rate by broad occupational classes. Clearly the probability of becoming unemployed increases significantly as the apparent skill level declines. Moreover as can be seen from the data, the duration of unemployment is significantly greater for the UK at all skill levels, while in both countries the duration is increasingly related to the skill level. Unlike developments in the USA, EFTA and Japan, the rise in unemployment in the European Union countries has been associated with a massive increase in long term unemployment.

Table 8
Unemployment by Skill : Flow & Duration
Britain & USA

<table>
<tr><th></th><th colspan="3">Britain (1984)</th><th colspan="3">USA (1987)</th></tr>
<tr><th></th><th>Inflow rate (% per mo.)</th><th>Average duration (mos.)</th><th>Unemploy-ment rate (%)</th><th>Inflow rate (% per mo.)</th><th>Average duration (mos.)</th><th>Unemploy-ment rate (%)</th></tr>
<tr><td>Professional & managerial</td><td>0.50</td><td>11.2</td><td>5.3</td><td>0.74</td><td>3.0</td><td>2.3</td></tr>
<tr><td>Clerical</td><td>0.88</td><td>10.1</td><td>8.0</td><td rowspan="2">1.58</td><td rowspan="2">2.6</td><td rowspan="2">4.3</td></tr>
<tr><td>Other non-manual</td><td>1.14</td><td>11.8</td><td>12.2</td></tr>
<tr><td>Skilled manual</td><td>1.02</td><td>14.2</td><td>12.6</td><td>1.97</td><td>2.9</td><td>6.1</td></tr>
<tr><td>Personal services</td><td rowspan="2">1.32</td><td rowspan="2">14.1</td><td rowspan="2">15.5</td><td>2.96</td><td>2.4</td><td>7.7</td></tr>
<tr><td>Other Manual</td><td>2.84</td><td>3.0</td><td>9.4</td></tr>
<tr><td>All</td><td>0.94</td><td>12.8</td><td>10.8</td><td>2.23</td><td>2.6</td><td>6.2</td></tr>
</table>

Source: Layard, Nickell & Jackman, *Unemployment*, 1991

It is impossible within the confines of this essay to deal adequately with the many problems with which unemployment presents us. The focus here is on what are the important issues for the next decade, and this is clearly one of them. In order to say something further about what we may expect, however, it is necessary to offer some brief explanation of the facts as we have observed them. Prognostication requires us to consider macro-economic factors, the behaviour of labour markets, changes in industrial structure and possible changes in the nature of work.

As a starting point it is useful to adopt the idea that there is in a sense an 'equilibrium' rate of unemployment to which in the longer run an economy will tend, given existing economic policies, current technology and the present state of economic and social institutions. This notion of an equilibrium rate of unemployment has been interpreted in different ways. In some analyses it is the rate of unemployment at which the supply and demand for labour come into balance in the long run. This is however a somewhat restrictive idea since the evidence suggests that labour markets in general adjust very slowly. A more general view that we will take here, is whether you accept labour market clearing or not, equilibrium unemployment can be interpreted as that rate of unemployment at which the inflation rate is stable (something described in the jargon as NAIRU, the non-accelerating inflation rate level of unemployment!) Note that at this equilibrium rate of unemployment the inflation rate is *stable* not necessarily *zero*. What the stable inflation rate is at equilibrium depends on the relationship between the rate of growth of the supply of money and the growth of real output.

This starting point suggests three significant questions. The first is that given the observed facts, why does unemployment fluctuate? The second is what determines the equilibrium level of unemployment itself, in the way in which we have defined it? The third question follows on from the second. If the unemployment rate is trending upward over a significant period of time this suggests that the rise in unemployment is not cyclical, which in turn implies that the equilibrium rate of unemployment is rising. The third question clearly is why?

Fluctuations in the unemployment level round its equilibrium result from shocks to the economic system. Such shocks may be characterised as demand shocks, supply shocks and policy shocks.

Demand shocks should be defined as autonomous shifts in spending behaviour by private economic agents. An apparently unexplained loss of business confidence might cause a collapse in private investment. Such shocks must be distinguished from an unanticipated change in demand brought about by, say, public spending. These are policy shocks not demand shocks. Shocks originating from the decisions of private agents were what the great Keynes was primarily concerned with in his seminal General Theory. Given the failure of the private sector to spend he advocated public expenditure, in particular public investment, to fill the gap created by the decline in private investment and its effects.[8]

Looking at the history of the world since the inception of the BNAC, it is difficult to identify major demand shocks of the kind that Keynes was concerned with. The rise in oil prices in 1973 and 1978, and their fall in 1986, are supply shocks, which altered the real cost base of industry and had significant effects on the terms of trade for individual countries. The period since 1969 has also been affected by major policy shocks - the major injection of inflation by governments after the end of Bretton Woods, the expansion of the US fiscal deficit in the eighties and the relaxation of world monetary policy after the stock market collapses of 1987. The conclusion is that supply shocks and policy shocks have largely been responsible for the macro-economic changes that have resulted in major and cyclical changes in unemployment. Stability in unemployment rates in the short run therefore depends on the ability of governments to avoid the de-stabilising macro-economic policies of the past, and on the (unforeseeable) absence of major supply side shocks. While these issues are important in determining the future paths of output and employment their analysis helps us little in dealing with our two remaining questions.

Deviations in the unemployment rate from equilibrium may be caused by shifts in demand as we have seen, although our conclusion is that this accounts for little of the actual behaviour of unemployment over the last two decades. It is clear however that whatever the differences in interpretation of 'equilibrium' unemployment, it is determined entirely by long- term supply factors. These factors include: the fiscal framework of taxes and subsidies, including unemployment benefits, the environment of training and search assistance for the unemployed, the prevailing technology and the behaviour of relevant social and economic institutions such as trades unions. Differences in these factors between countries have been found to account for something of the order of 90 per cent of their observed differences in unemployment rates over the long term.[9]

---

[8] J M Keynes. *The General Theory of Employment, Interest and Money,* MacMillan 1936
[9] See Layard, Nickell and Jackman *op cit* p. 55

It is impossible to be comprehensive with regard to the specific determinants of equilibrium rates of unemployment. But taking into account the variables enumerated there is little doubt as to what the principal factors appear to be. They are, the nature of the benefit system, the organisation of economic institutions, particularly trades unions, and the infrastructure that determines manpower policy. The actual behaviour of unemployment is complicated by the nature of unemployment dynamics. Whatever the origins of unemployment, the actual rate of unemployment may from time to time exhibit a life of its own. This is reflected in the conduct and nature of job search procedures. For example, the longer the duration of unemployment the less likely is the unemployed to get a job. Thus, comparing the UK and the US, the inflow into unemployment is not significantly different -but the long duration of the unemployed in the UK translates a similar inflow into a much larger pool. A process of "hysteresis" sets in that is quite independent of the original cause of the unemployment.

One way of approaching the supply side aspect of sustained unemployment and a relatively high equilibrium level of employment is to pose the following question. If equilibrium employment as defined above does not imply that everyone who wants a job can get one, i.e. labour markets will clear, why don't they?

The simple answer is that the level of real wages remains at a level above which the buyers and sellers are matched, but this is mere tautology. The reason it remains above that level is either the fact that for some reason employers are willing and content to pay such a price despite the willingness of the unemployed to work at a lower real wage, or that those offering themselves for work persistently demand such a price, despite the existence of unemployment, or some combination of the two.

On the side of the individual employer it is sometimes argued that it is in his interest to pay above the market clearing rate in order to maintain high morale, and attract superior labour. This is described as the 'efficiency wage' argument. It is also said to encourage recruitment and to give the firm an image as a 'good payer'. The trouble with this argument is that while it may be plausible for one employer in isolation it does not explain why this should result in a *general* level of real wages that is above the market clearing rate.

On the side of the employee there are several compelling reasons why the real wage demanded may persistently exceed the market clearing level. The first in a number of countries has been the power of trades unions and its progressive impact on labour market behaviour from the seventies onwards. It is often (today more often) correctly said that trades unions do not create inflation, but they can create unemployment. In so far as inflation is ultimately a monetary phenomenon this is indeed the case. Unlike the situation in the US, this has been a particular problem in Europe, where over three-quarters of the workforce has been historically subjected to collective bargaining. This process is reinforced by the difference in power exercised by those in work *versus* those out of work, the so-called insider/outsider problem. Trade union commitment is primarily for insiders *versus* outsiders. It is for them that they negotiate. It should also be noted that insider power will be greater in systems of union organisation where negotiations tend to be on a direct employer basis rather than on an industry or national basis.

The other principal factor that may prevent market clearing is simply an unwillingness to accept work at the market clearing wage. The most common reason for this, which also explains much of the difference between European Union and United States unemployment behaviour, is the nature of the benefit system. In Europe there is little doubt that generous benefit systems, both in terms of the benefit/wage (replacement ratio) and the duration of unemployment benefit both diminish job search and reduce the acceptability of alternative employment. Sand is thrown into the market adjustment mechanism. Moreover it is not simply a matter of accepting or not accepting the going rate at the margin in a preferred occupation. The existence of benefit may discourage the transfer to another. Unemployment rates in the United States since the middle seventies relative to the European Union have clearly benefited from the transfer of much labour from relatively highly paid jobs in contracting and manufacturing industry to the more lowly paid expanding service sector. This has not happened in Europe on the same scale, which in part must be due to the generosity of unemployment relief.

The third question asks why in some countries the equilibrium level of unemployment has risen, particularly in the European Union, and in the other countries apparently less. The answer appears to lie in part in the persistence of the effects (historically) of powerful trades unions plus generous benefit systems which have reduced labour market flexibility, which as argued affects the equilibrium level of unemployment. It also influences the change in the equilibrium level through the dynamic process outlined earlier, namely unless a rise in unemployment is rapidly reversed it can generate its own dynamics resulting in a large overhang of semi-permanent or long term unemployed. While there is little doubt that this is a major part of the story, there is a further set of considerations that are prayed in aid to account for what we see and to speculate about the future.

The structure of output is changing, across the OECD. Illustrative figures for the major players are given in Table 9. It can be seen that in general across the major traditional industrial countries the share of manufacturing output and employment are declining. In some countries, notably the United States and the United Kingdom, much concern has been expressed about the developments. A recent study of employment trends in the United Kingdom began with the words

> "A critical policy issue for maintaining employment is that of halting or reversing the decline of the UK's comparative advantage in manufacturing"[10].

Table 9
The Distribution of Total Output

	1960	1970	1980	1985	1990
USA					
Manufacturing	28.3	25.7	21.8	20.1	19.3*
Services	57.9	62.5	63.5	66.9	68.8*
Other Industry	13.8	11.8	14.7	13.0	11.9
JAPAN					
Manufacturing	34.6	35.9	29.2	29.5	28.9
Services	42.7	47.3	54.4	55.8	55.7
Other Industry	22.7	16.8	16.4	14.7	15.4
E.C.					
Manufacturing	32.4	30.3	26.5	24.7	23.3
Services	47.7	52.9	58.5	61.4	64.4
Other Industry	19.9	16.8	15.0	13.9	12.3
U.K.					
Manufacturing	32.1	33.4	23.2	20.7	19.6*
Services	53.8	60.0	61.5	63.8	69.2
Other Industry	14.1	12.8	15.3	15.5	11.2*
WEST GERMANY					
Manufacturing	40.3	38.4	32.4	31.7	30.8
Services	41.0	47.4	55.5	57.7	59.2
Other Industry	18.7	14.2	12.1	10.6	10.0
CANADA					
Manufacturing	23.3	20.4	17.9	17.2	17.3
Services	60.0	64.6	63.2	65.7	67.3
Other Industry	16.7	15.0	18.9	17.1	15.4

*1987 latest data

Source: OECD Historical Statistics, 1960-1990, OECD Paris
OECD National Accounts, 1971-1991, OECD Paris

[10] C Greenalgh, *Employment and Structural Change in Britain: Trends and Options,* The Employment Institute, December 1989, p. 3

Taken literally this statement is simply silly. Other versions of it abound in other places. It is not possible for relative improvements to contribute to general improvements in economic growth and job creation. We are not playing a zero-sum game. However, there are potentially serious issues that do arise from the changes in output structure that have taken place and are likely to continue in the future.

We start with the prediction that the trends observed in Table 9 will continue. The potential for increases in manufacturing productivity in the OECD is such that it will match and almost certainly rise faster than the real demand for manufactures. Both technology and the structure of final demand will not allow the hands of the clock to be turned back. Technology provides the basis for productivity improvement while changes in the structure of final demand will continue to move in the direction of the service based economy. The description 'service' is itself misleading because it implies a dependence on another form of economic activity i.e. manufacturing. But service products are themselves now complex, and much of manufacturing industry (the computer industry for example) is heavily dependent on service producers.

Insofar as this is the case we may be presented with a substantial problem of adjustment as business structure changes. To a large extent this has already happened in the United States, where high paid manufacturing unskilled jobs have been replaced by low paid service jobs. The adjustment process elsewhere in the OECD has not and will not be so easily accomplished. Changes in technology and the changing structure of demand will mean a continuing diminishing role for the semi-skilled and unskilled worker in manufacturing industry across the major industrial players in the OECD over the next decade.

The unemployment problem, as it is currently perceived, is unlikely to be assisted by changing demographics. While growth in the labour forces in the major industrial countries is likely to slow in the next decade, neither this nor a return to the growth rate of the last decade will themselves make much impact on unemployment rates. Such changes as may be looked for, where they are possible, must come from changes on the supply side of economies. This particularly applies to the members of the European Union, whose social policies are largely responsible for the Union's poor unemployment performance relative to the United States, EFTA and Japan. These changes require a reform of benefit systems, a reduction in the power of trades unions and positive manpower training and other policies.[11] The Social Chapter of the

Maastricht Treaty, if implemented, will simply contribute to a rise in the unemployment rate of the Union.

Labour market policies have clearly been given less attention by the large industrial countries than should have been the case. The model country in this respect has been seen to be Sweden. Benefits for the unemployed cease after 14 months, but linked to this are labour market policies designed to help people to find productive work. They involve the use of placement services, retraining and reinvestment subsidies based on a six month period. In addition temporary work is available in the public sector. The package is expensive, costing the Swedish tax payer one per cent of GDP. But there is an offset in unemployment benefits and in the long term are not far from being self-financing.

Sadly, however, even in this case, the general approach has broken down. At the time of writing, core unemployment in Sweden has risen to 10%, close to the European Union average. The fundamental fact has to be faced - that there is very little longer term alternative to the reality of improving labour market flexibility as compared with trying to compensate for its inefficiency. More recent advocates within the Clinton administration in the United States, that are recommending minimum wage legislation and greater employee protection, are simply preparing the ground for greater problems in creating employment than has been the case in the past. North America has nothing to learn from Europe in this respect. There is simply a serious danger that it will import its disease.

The employment/unemployment problem is often posed in the context of the question, 'where are the jobs coming from'? This may turn out to be a rather unhelpful way to approach the problem in the long run. Given the unlimited capacity of consumers to consume, not particular products, but to enjoy more consumption in general, the problem of unemployment is essentially a problem about markets. Why do markets fail, if they do, to reconcile the availability of human resources with human desires? ('Needs' has too narrow a connotation.) That is the question we should continually seek to address.

If this is correct much of the speculation about the future of work, schemes to reduce unemployment by early retirement and schemes for work sharing to deal with the perceived problem of unemployment are at best attempts to treat

---

[11] On the issue of education and training, note, Frederick W Crawford and Simon Webley "Continuing Education and Training for the Workforce", *BNAC Issues Paper No 1*. 1992

the symptoms of the problem rather than the disease. The question of the future nature of work is beyond the scope of this paper. One can see the logic of the distinction between core and peripheral employment and can expect that large organisations will over the next decade divest themselves, or 'privatise' many of their functions, but the impact of such changes on overall labour market behaviour is hard to divine. Early retirement, apart from the inherent resource waste, runs up against a growing problem, referred to in the next section, namely the coming importance of the Third Age. Work sharing is simply a clumsy device for income sharing which is clearly inferior to a simple employment subsidy derived from taxation - if income sharing is what you wish to achieve.

Clearly, this is a contentious area. Some see the "artificial" generation of work as simply a temporary phenomenon, accepting the fact that in some sense in the longer term markets will sort matters out. Some see the whole nature of work changing in response to unemployment pressures, with greater flexibility in institutional/labour contractual relations. Others see a significant expansion in the voluntary sector as part of an employment response. The key issue, however, remains to what extent do we see high unemployment rates in the OECD simply reflecting slow rates of labour market adjustment that will eventually restore equilibrium, as contrasted with a major structural change or changes that have left a substantial proportion of the labour force unemployable in a conventional sense.

7. Public Finance and the Role of the State

In 1969 Harry Johnson regarded the potential problems raised by public expenditure and taxation as 'awesome'. Since Johnson wrote, as can be seen from Tables 10, 11 and 12, public expenditure in the G7 countries as a proportion of gross domestic product has risen significantly, as have public sector financial deficits and the ratios of national debt to GDP. On the basis of these measures, the role of the state since 1969 has increased, but in a number of instances, beginning in the eighties, the role of the state in other respects has been reduced through the process of privatisation. The role of governments as taxers and spenders has increased, while in a number of cases the role of government as manager has declined.

Table 10
Government Expenditure as % of GDP
(current disbursements)

	1960-67	1968-73	1974-79	1980-90
CANADA	25.4	31.0	35.8	42.0
UK	30.8	33.2	39.6	41.7
USA	25.8	29.1	31.2	34.7
EC	29.1	32.4	39.0	44.5
OECD	25.9	28.6	33.4	37.9

Source: Historical Statistics, 1960-90, OECD, Paris

Conventional wisdom in the early seventies, particularly in the Anglo-Saxon and Scandinavian countries, placed much emphasis on the role of fiscal policy in steering the economy and maintaining full employment. The primacy of fiscal policy for this purpose arose in part from the intellectual influence of Keynes and in part from the technical issue that under Bretton Woods with a pegged exchange rate system, fiscal policy could be used to influence nominal demand whereas monetary policy could not (since it was committed to the task of stabilising the exchange rate). After Bretton Woods, under a floating exchange rate system, the roles were reversed. In a world of floating rates and perfectly mobile capital it is monetary policy that becomes the senior partner with fiscal policy relegated to a much less significant role. Attempts by a number of European countries (most significantly the United Kingdom, Italy and Sweden) to avoid the recession of 1974–5 by increased deficit financing, resulted in near disaster, and in the case of the United Kingdom ended in the arrival of the brokers' men from the IMF in 1976. This episode, when coupled with the unfortunate experience of West Germany in 1978 in attempting to lead Europe out of impending recession, put a considerable damper on the idea of the importance of active stabilisation policy, and the role of fiscal policy in particular. In theory at any rate, governments began to eschew what beliefs they had in the use of discretionary fiscal policy to manage demand. Economic debates on the matter continue. There are those who put forward reasons why the long term impact of fiscal changes on demand is likely to be negligible, those who believe that the principal role of fiscal policy is to provide an appropriate fiscal framework to encourage the supply side of the economy, and those who still to some degree hanker after the old ideas that would see fiscal policy as a significant tool in the armoury of short term economic management.

Table 11

General government Financial Balances as % of Nominal GDP

Surplus (+) or Deficit (-)

	CANADA	FRANCE	GERMANY	JAPAN	UK	USA
1970	-4.0	+1.1	+0.2	+1.7	+2.9	-1.1
1980	-2.8	0.0	-2.9	-4.4	-3.4	-1.3
1985	-6.8	-2.9	-1.2	-0.8	-2.9	-3.1
1986	-5.4	-2.7	-1.3	-0.9	-2.4	-3.4
1987	-3.8	-1.9	-1.9	+0.5	-1.3	-2.5
1988	-2.5	-1.7	-2.2	+1.5	+1.0	-2.0
1989	-3.0	-1.3	+0.1	+2.5	+0.9	-1.5
1990	-4.1	-1.5	-2.0	+2.9	-1.3	-2.5
1991	-6.1	-2.1	-3.2	+3.0	-2.9	-3.4
1992	-6.4	-3.9	-2.8	+1.8	-6.7	-4.7

Source: *OECD Economic Outlook, June 1993*

Historically the idea of deficit financing that followed the publication of Keynes' General Theory was criticised by many as being financially irresponsible. It was objected to on the grounds that a prudent government should balance its books as between taxation and spending. Borrowing and increasing the national debt it was said was inequitable since it represented borrowing by the present generation to be paid off by the next - it created a burden for our children. Moreover such borrowings and the interest payable on them could not be dealt with by ever rising taxes, and eventually the pressure on government would be resolved by printing money and imposing an inflation tax on the lenders.

Table 12
Gross Public Debt
(as % of Nominal GDP)

	1981	1983	1985	1986	1987	1988	1989	1990	1991	1992
CANADA	45.1	56.1	65.0	68.9	70.1	69.3	69.5	71.9	77.6*	83.0
FRANCE	36.4	41.4	45.4	45.7	47.2	46.8	47.5	46.6	48.6	51.6*
GERMANY	36.3	41.0	42.5	42.5	43.8	44.4	43.2	43.6*	42.0	43.2*
ITALY	61.0	72.0	84.3	88.2	92.6	94.8	97.9	100.5	104.0*	108.1
JAPAN	57.1	66.5	68.7	72.3	74.9	72.8	70.6	69.8	68.2*	66.2*
UK	54.5	53.1	52.7	51.1	48.6	42.2	36.8	34.7	36.4	41.0*
USA	37.2	44.3	48.3	51.3	52.6	53.2	54.0	56.2	59.8	63.2*
TOTAL MAJOR 7 COUNTRIES	44.5	51.6	55.5	57.9	59.4	59.0	58.6	59.5	61.2	63.3

Source: *OECD Economic Outlook, June 1993*

*from this year, data are OECD estimates

The response to this involved several arguments in mitigation. The first was that deficit financing was to be a cyclical phenomenon. Government would balance its books, but over the business cycle, not in every year. Governments would alternately run deficits and surpluses as the state of aggregate demand dictated in order to smooth out fluctuations, but there would be no tendency for debt to rise in the long run. Secondly even if debt did rise, leaving aside the complication that some part of the national debt might be held overseas, this did not create a burden for future generations since the benefit to future receivers of interest would offset the burden on future taxpayers. Society as a whole would be neither better nor worse off. Finally both these (predominantly) pre-Second World War arguments were overtaken by a post-war argument put forward by the American economist Evesy Domar. Domar argued that what mattered was not the absolute level of the debt in the long run, but its ratio to gross domestic product. The financial effect of increasing public debt and society's ability to service it, depended said Domar on the debt ratio. Provided that the debt ratio remained stable it was possible to enjoy not only the short term benefits of demand smoothing through deficit financing, but also the benefits (such as they were seen to be) of a growing public sector - provided that that sector did not grow more rapidly in terms of debt than the economy as a whole. This analysis did not of course resolve one crucial issue - namely what determines, or how do you go about, determining what the optimal debt ratio for society should be?[12]

Domar's analysis focussed on one important technical point. Suppose that a borrower is faced with an interest rate that is above the rate of growth of his income. Unless he makes an effort to service his loan by repaying some principal i.e. by reducing the so-called "primary" deficit, excluding interest, the loan increases each year by the addition of increased charges, if he also has to borrow the interest. If there is no debt servicing whatever, the growth rate of the debt is the interest rate. It follows that since the interest rate is above the growth rate of income, debt would be increasing faster than income and the debt/income ratio rises. This phenomenon has been a characteristic of many countries during the eighties when real interest rates have exceeded real rates of growth. The rise in debt ratios is exhibited in Table 12. Table 13 shows real rates of growth and real rates of interest for selected periods since 1970 for the countries shown. The rise in real interest rates in the eighties has clearly been a significant factor in increasing the burden of sovereign debt.

This rise in sovereign debt ratios in various countries in the eighties has been largely mirrored in the private sector. Both personal and corporate debt in the UK and North America rose sharply, as can be seen in Table 14.

These increases in indebtedness of all kinds during the eighties have led to speculation that the nineties will be essentially a period of severe disinflation as the burdens of debt are reduced by a lower rate of net borrowing and therefore, spending. This will inhibit economic growth through the period, it is said, until balance sheets are brought closer to some sort of equilibrium. An alternative and equally gloomy view is that it is only through a return to some form of inflationary environment that the real burden of debt will actually be reduced. However, one thing is certain, namely that the high level of real

---

[12] E.D. Domar, "The Burden of Debt and The National Income," *American Economic Review,* vol 34, no 4, December, 1944, pp. 798-827. Reprinted as chap. 2 in E.D. Domar, *Essays in the Theory of Economic Growth,* Oxford University Press, New York, 1957

interest rates (at the time of writing) makes the process difficult, and it will take some time. The widespread increase in debt must remain a cause for concern, although whether it poses a severe threat to the integrity of the financial system remains a matter for debate.[13]

Table 13

The deterioration in the relationship between interest rates and growth rates 1960-1990

	GNP/GDP	Real long term interest rates	Growth/Interest differential (%)
USA			
1968-73	3.2	0.6	+2.6
1974-79	2.4	-0.6	+3.0
1980-90	2.6	5.4	-2.8
JAPAN			
1968-73	8.6	0.4	+8.2
1974-79	3.6	0.0	+3.6
1980-90	4.1	4.6	-0.5
WEST GERMANY			
1968-73	4.9	2.1	+2.8
1974-79	2.3	3.0	-0.7
1980-90	2.0	4.5	-2.5
UK			
1968-73	3.4	2.0	+1.4
1974-79	1.5	-2.0	+3.5
1980-90	2.1	3.5	-1.4
CANADA			
1968-73	5.4	2.2	+3.2
1974-79	4.2	0.0	+4.2
1980-90	2.8	5.9	-3.1
FRANCE			
1968-73	5.4	1.6	+3.8
1974-79	2.8	-0.4	+3.2
1980-90	2.1	5.0	-2.9

Source: Historical Statistics, 1960-90, OECD, Paris

[13] On the question of global financial stability see H B Rose "The Changing World of Finance and its Problems", *BNAC Issues Paper No 2*, March 1993

In the case of sovereign debt the argument partly turns on whether it is thought that present debt levels are sustainable. At the level of sovereign debt it is arguable that up to a totally unacceptable (if unpreventable?) rate of inflation deficits may be sustained by the ability of governments to issue money. That process, accompanied by inflation, may continue for some time. Moreover any given debt ratio may be sustained given the willingness of the citizens to pay sufficient taxes to keep it there. These two thoughts may give us some clue as to how to define an appropriate debt ratio and public sector borrowing requirement. A given debt ratio is both appropriate and sustainable if it is consistent with some equilibrium between public expenditure (including interest payments) and the willingness of the public to pay taxes, obviating the need for the government to attempt to monetise the debt. This does not of course require that the budget so defined should be balanced. This argument can be applied to the fiscal deficit as a proportion of gross domestic product. Given the rate of growth of income and a given ratio of the fiscal deficit to income, there is only one debt ratio at which the debt ratio will be stable. For example, if the fiscal deficit to income ratio is 2 per cent and the growth rate of income is 3 per cent, the debt ratio will stabilise at 66per cent, as 3 per cent of 66 is 2 per cent. If people are unwilling (or are perceived to be unprepared) to pay taxes such that either public sector borrowing is crowding out private spending, and/or an inflation tax is being used to finance expenditure and reduce the real level of public debt, the financial deficit and its associated stable debt ratio are too high. The practical problem is to determine where that point is. Given the current state of the public finances of the principal players in the OECD at the present time this is an issue of prime importance.

This analysis may be supplemented by the addition of what has come to be known as the "Golden Rule", which has been focussed on in several continental European countries, including Germany in the past. In simple terms, the argument says that current consumption by government should be financed out of taxation and other income received, while new assets may be legitimately financed from borrowings. Accordingly, the public sector borrowing requirement would be equal to public sector investment. In applying this rule, account needs to be taken of the cyclical implications of public sector borrowing behaviour due to the operation of the so-called built-in stabilisers.

The importance of the question is magnified by the prospective pressures on public spending and taxation that are likely to prevail into the next century. Twenty-five years ago Harry Johnson foresaw the concern that spread later with regard to the nature of taxation. Already there were concerns about the inequity, onerous nature and disincentive offsets of the tax system. To a substantial extent these concerns were recognised in the eighties with a tendency to reduce taxation, particularly at the higher income levels, across several countries. Such changes were by no means universally welcomed and they came as part of the trend toward de-regulating markets, and promoting enterprise, whose future we discuss later. Moreover, where revenues have fallen as a result (or been lower than they would otherwise have been) they have not been matched by declines in public spending, with the consequence for debt ratios that we have already seen.

Table 14
Private Sector Indebtedness

	Corporate Sector as a % of GNP/GDP	**Households as a % of disposable income**
CANADA		
1980	68	85
1985	67	73
1989	71	87
WEST GERMANY		
1980	69	76
1985	73	88
1989	74	87
JAPAN		
1980	86	58
1985	101	68
1989	130	92
UK		
1980	40	48
1985	47	76
1989	80	105
USA		
1980	34	77
1985	39	83
1989	48	96

Source: Bank for International Settlements, 61st annual report, p. 61 (Basle 1991)

Against this change in the revenue background, compounded recently by the cyclical effects of recession, the demand for public spending has risen unabated. In 1969 Johnson wrote:

> "...there has been some questioning of whether the functions that have been assumed by the state in respect of social security, medical care, and so forth - essentially as a result of 1930's conceptions of the responsibilities of the state to the individual - continue to be appropriate in a more literate professional and privately wealthy society. Re-definition of the appropriate distribution of responsibility between the individual and the state, and reform of the tax system to reconcile the needs of the state for revenue with the needs of the economy for equity and efficiency in public finance, will definitely be high on the agenda for each country in the coming decade". (Johnson *op cit* p. 21)

Unfortunately this is still true today - except that the need is even greater. The insatiable appetite of the voters for the promises of the politician (the cost of which will be naturally borne by someone else!) will continue. The big-ticket items remain remorselessly the same, education, the cost of health, the economic welfare of the disadvantaged and the cost of preserving the environment. People have their own private lists of issues and causes. To these must be added the problems that are to be with us in the form of the so-called Third Age and after: an inexorable rise in the ratio of elderly and retired people to the working population. That change, widely to be experienced, interacts with both the cost of health and the problem of the economic welfare of the elderly.

Forecasts of the age structure of the population of several leading countries are given in Table 15. They can only be regarded as indicative, but they make it clear, that on present trends in fertility and mortality, the populations of those listed will become progressively older. In thirty years' time, over a fifth of the populations of Germany and Japan will be over 65. Table 16 sets out the changes expected in the dependency ratio for the same countries, defined as the young (<14) and the old (>65) as a percentage of the working age group 15–64. These changes will have significant consequences for the patterns of social expenditure on health, education and pensions.[14]

With health costs (public and private) already accounting for over 14 per cent of gross national product in the United States, it is clear that the cost of health both there and elsewhere will be a major issue over the next decade.

---

[14] R S Belous, "Demographic Currents: Trends & Issues that Face the United States, the United Kingdom and Canada", *BNAC Occasional Paper No 7.*, September 1991

Table 15
Age Structures of Populations, 1980 - 2050 (%)

	Age	1980	2000	2020	2040	2050
USA	15 - 64	66	67	65	61	62
	65+	11	12	16	19	19
UK	15 - 64	64	65	64	62	62
	65+	15	14	16	20	19
CANADA	15 - 64	68	68	64	59	60
	65+	10	13	16	22	21
JAPAN	15 - 64	67	67	62	60	60
	65+	9	15	21	23	23
GERMANY	15 - 64	66	67	65	57	59
	65+	16	18	22	28	24

Sources: OECD demographic data file; 1980 actual numbers; all other years based on OECD demographic model (medium fertility variant projections)

Table 16
Dependency Ratios, 1980-2050*

	1980	2000	2020	2040	2050
USA	51.1	51.6	49.8	62.4	62.5
UK	56.2	51.9	53.8	61.9	60.2
CANADA	48.1	47.4	47.9	66.5	67.7
JAPAN	48.4	42.2	48.6	59.5	65.7
GERMANY	50.8	44.0	48.3	68.7	69.9

*The dependency ratio is calculated as follows:
[Population (0-14) + Population (65+)/Population (15-64)] x 100

Sources: OECD demographic data file; 1980 actual numbers; all other years based on OECD demographic model (medium fertility variant projections).

Given the current state of the public finances of the major OECD players, it is difficult to see how the various problems will be coped with, without the re-examination of traditional methods of delivery and the 're-definition' of the appropriate definition of responsibilities between the individual and the state that Johnson called for so long ago. It no longer appears to be enough to contemplate marginal changes in tax systems and small changes in public spending. A process of rebalancing the relationship between the individual and the state, and privatising the use of resources is the only way to try and establish some consistency between stability in public finances and delivering what is collectively needed.

The worldwide move in the direction of privatisation is at least one step in transforming the relationship between the public and the private sector. In many respects and in many countries this reduces the role of the state in areas of business life and economic activity, where *qua* government it has little competence. Developments of this kind are likely to continue. The motives for this are mixed. Some governments perceive privatisation as a short- term source of revenue. Others focus on the potential economic and social gain to be obtained from the more efficient use of resources and the relief to government, enabling it to focus more clearly on those decisions that only it can make. While talk of the end of history goes too far, what is happening is itself a kind of revolution that for the foreseeable future is unlikely to be reversed. Against this background, we may recall the wise words of Adam Smith:

> "In every great monarchy of Europe the sale of crown lands would produce a very large sum of money, which, if applied to the payment of public debts, would deliver from mortgage much greater revenues than any which those lands have ever afforded the crown."[15]

The reduction of the role of the state as manager has however been matched to a large extent by the expansion of the role of the state as regulator. While privatisation may be seen as an extension of the role of private enterprise as a manager of economic resources, the extension of regulation may reflect the introduction of socialism by the back door. The prime function of regulation is to deal with the problem of market failure - the chronic inability of the market place to deliver the sort of signals that encourage the joint achievement of appropriate social benefits and private gains. There is however a grave danger that in many markets and activities regulatory activities are not designed to fulfil this function, but instead impose behaviour

[15] A. Smith, *Wealth of Nations* (Glasgow edn. 1776), Oxford: Clarendon Press, 1976

patterns that reflect specific value judgements and moral imperatives. The problem is compounded when such regulatory activities at the same time seek to recoup the cost of such activities and their consequences from private agents. This has potentially serious consequences for business (which are clearly substantially with us) and for economic performance over the next decade.

The late Harry Johnson foresaw this problem clearly in another paper written for the BNAC in 1973 which addressed the problem of the environment from an economic point of view.[16] The regulation of the environment and the promotion of environmental control will continue to be of major significance. Johnson and more recent commentators such as David Pearce would have agreed that there are two major problems related to the issue of environmental control. The first is the widespread existence of disputes between scientific authorities with regard to the interpretation of such facts as are available with regard to phenomena such as global warming and worldwide population growth.

The second is more closely associated with Johnson's interest - the relationship between environmental and economic issues. Oversimplifying, the argument as put by David Pearce criticises the attempts by the environmental lobbies to influence politicians and decision makers by concentrating on moral imperatives that have little weight.[17] Pearce goes on to argue that there is a significant economic calculus that can be applied to justify various types of environmental policy, and it is only by applying that calculus that ultimately politicians and public opinion can be influenced. It has to be established that economic benefit and environmental protection go hand in hand rather than existing as alternatives as many believe. There may in certain circumstances be a trade off between the two but there are important complementarities. The danger is that the environmental lobbies supported by government regulation will impose costs on economic activity that in the long run will turn into a major social loss of welfare. This issue presents a serious problem for business, governments, and communities at large both now and in the foreseeable future.

---

[16] See H G Johnson "Man and His Environment", 1973 re-issued as *BNAC Occasional Paper No 6*, June 1990

[17] D Pearce, "Conserving global national wealth: economics and politics" in *The Economics of Wealth Creation* edited by James Ball, Edward Elgar, 1992

8. The Behaviour of Nations (The Industrial World)

Economics is political economy. Economic events and the formation and conduct of economic policies take place within a political framework. That political framework influences both domestically and internationally through relationships between nations. It was argued earlier that a powerful motive for United States support for a free trade world after the Second World War was derived from considerations of American foreign policy and national security. Except obliquely in the discussion of trade, no consideration has been paid in the previous sections to the economic significance of global political change. Indeed it is difficult to map ideas of such change into economic specifics - even before allowing for the inherently speculative nature of such ideas themselves.

We may start from the point made earlier and exhibited in Table 6 that, since the BNAC started, the balance of economic power in the OECD countries has continued to change. Perhaps the most significant characteristic of the world in which we now live is the change in the balance of economic power between the United States, Europe (in the widest sense) and Japan and the rest of Asia. It must, however, be remembered that the United States in a statistical sense is still the wealthiest country in the world by far and with the exception of oil, the only major country that could exist on the basis of self-sufficiency. Even that constraint might be modified by adding Canada (which in effect is already there through the free trade agreement) and possibly Mexico further down the road. But while the relative economic position of the United States has declined, up to now at least, the Pax Americana has continued. The security of the Western world *versus* the East continued to rest on the military strength and capability of America. But the issue is more general, as the Gulf War has illustrated. At this stage still only the United States was able to mount and lead the kind of effort that was required.

However, as we shall see clearly in the next section, the change in the balance of economic power within the major industrial countries is only a part of a significant change in the pattern of world economic growth and output. Here we focus on the position of the leading economic players, the European Union, Japan, and the United States. In the next section we look at developments taking place in the rest of the world.

The apparent ending of a coherent threat from Communism in the East, associated with the reunification of Germany, raises the whole question of the need for the Pax Americana, and the willingness of America to provide it. It has been argued that the removal of that threat brings with it as many problems as it has removed. In a sense its existence, like the Bretton Woods agreement with regard to exchange rates, imposed a coherence on national behaviour that is no longer there. The consequence of this, it is said, is to provide the possibility of greater local instability in relations between countries, in the East as in what was Yugoslavia, and in other parts of the world where Islamic fundamentalism is a major issue. Clearly the response of the United States to these changes in the world political scene and the attitudes of the major players to the United States are a matter of crucial importance to the economic as well as the political relations between nations over the next decade. The danger is a reversion on all fronts to a world of the thirties, in which both international political and international economic co-operation were minimal, partly because of the isolationism of the United States.

It must also be appreciated that the ending of the Cold War and subsequent developments create opportunities for the re-assessment of attitudes, not simply for the United States but also for the other major players, notably Germany and Japan.

Clearly it was United States policy after the Second World War to encourage and sustain economic recovery in both Germany and Japan in response to the Communist threat from both the Soviet Union and China. Strong support was given to the creation of the European Economic Community in 1957. In the context of the recent European debates about a federal Europe it is ironic to recall that the principal motivation for establishing it was not economic at all, but political. Although, as it turned out, its political significance was greatest in providing a bulwark against encroachment from the East, its principal purpose was to eliminate the possibility of a fourth war between France and Germany. Economic integration between the various states was seen by the founding fathers as a necessary prelude to longer term political stability.

The end of the Cold War, particularly the unification of Germany, opens up new questions about the future of the European Union at both economic and political levels. As a political entity, the Union acted as a significant cushion between East and West. Its role, on the face of it, is no longer necessary. Moreover, with the disappearance of what may be described as a security boundary, the question now arises as to where 'Europe' begins and 'Europe' ends. The very concept of Europe which had been narrowly defined in terms of the Union on the one hand and the so-called EFTA countries on the other is unclear. The meaning of the Union itself is open to re-definition with the application of countries such as Austria and Norway to become members. With the possible exception of Switzerland, it is reasonable to expect that the other members of EFTA might become members of the 'Union' by the end of the century. But this raises the further question of whether ambitions such as those contained in the Maastricht Treaty can be realised in this wider framework, especially in view of the likely desire of some Eastern European countries to become members of the Union.

While it is possible to see that the European Union as a framework for trading relationships may continue to be of significance, it is to be doubted whether the wider ambitions of the so-called pro-Europeans can be realised, including moves toward a single currency and some form of political federalism. The issue is, and will continue to be, much debated. Whatever the outcome, it must be accepted that the developments leading up to the proposals culminating in the Maastricht Treaty took place against a background of a very different geo-political world than the one we now inhabit. The move toward a so-called Single Market began a decade ago. The collapse of communism in Eastern Europe is barely five years old. The future of the Union must not only be re-examined in the light of its possible enlargement, it must be re-examined in the light of the implications of the re-unification of Germany, and the relationship of the new Germany to Eastern Europe. Looked at in this light the debates about the future of Europe taking place in countries like the United Kingdom and France are like the wars between the Lilliputians and the inhabitants of Brobdingnag - the big endians and the little endians, for the cognoscente of boiled eggs!

The re-unification of Germany, allied to the ending of the Cold War, means that in a significant respect the Second World War is at last now over. The geo-political framework in which we have lived and worked for nearly fifty years was shaped by the war itself and the international response to it after the war. In terms of both trade and politics, the components of what became, later, the German Empire historically faced East rather than West. The Western posture of Western Germany in both respects after the war was fostered by circumstance. It is no longer clear that, given the changes that have taken place, it will be seen to be in the interest of Germany to focus on the West and the institutional framework of the European Union, rather than to turn towards its traditional relationships with Eastern Europe. Of all the Union members, Germany has the best motivation and capability to take the lion's share of Eastern European markets as they develop. Thus Germany has the opportunity, which it will undoubtedly take, to re-define its position in the European Union as it stands and *vis-à-vis* Eastern Europe. The centre of gravity in Europe is bound to move eastwards. One can only say at this stage that it is unclear why Germany should have the commitment to a united Europe, either economically or politically, that has been in her interest in the past.

To some degree, the Japanese find themselves with a similar opportunity to re-define their role in the economic and political world. There are however significant differences between them. The similarity lies in the fact that with the end of the Cold War, Japan no longer needs the Pax Americana to defend herself from the Soviet Union. But her position is unlike that of Germany in major respects. The first is that unlike Germany the United States is a significant trading partner for Japan. The second is that unlike Germany, political behaviour in Japan since the war has been of very little consequence for the Japanese people and for the Japanese economy. Thirdly Japan is faced with a specific regional problem in the Pacific Rim, namely the rise in the economic power of China.

The first of these factors means that Japan still will not have the degree of independence from the United States that the Germans will enjoy. Their new found independence on the basis of security must be carefully traded off against the economic benefits of good relations. However there is no doubt that concerns about the ending of the Japanese economic miracle allied to the ending of the Cold War are resulting in a call for political reform in Japan and a re-definition of the position of Japan in the international polity. Demands for Japan to be responsible for her own security have begun to emerge. Volatile political developments such as these cannot be handled simply by MITI and the Keidenran. Government must become more capable and responsible. Finally, leaving aside the question of whether the Japanese economic miracle is over in the form that we have understood it, there remains the question of Japan's position in the Pacific Region, particularly *vis-à-vis* China.

To say that the Japanese economic miracle is over is not to imply some long term inability of Japan to grow at least as fast as other leading members of the OECD. It is to recognise that the economic strategy that Japan Inc. has been pursuing for the last quarter century is probably no longer viable. That strategy has consisted of pricing for market share, passing on increases in productivity to the consumer rather than the producer, and financing massive investments with cheap finance primarily from the banking system. The consequences as seen at present are unprofitable firms, increasingly unhappy workers who want to close the gap between rising productivity and their real standard of living, and a financial system, particularly the banking sector that, by Anglo-Saxon accounting standards, is effectively bust. A further consequence is a new and novel interest in the Japanese political system as noted above. Politicians are of little interest until things go wrong. Then they are expected to put everything right.

Japan's problems in the longer run may be compounded by the rise of China, which is discussed below. Here the point is that it may be expected that trading relations between China and the diaspora Chinese in the region will grow, especially after the acquisition of Hong Kong in 1997. There is a danger that Japan could become isolated between the United States as a major trading partner on the one hand, and a major Chinese based (in the broader sense) trading group in the Pacific Region.

As far as the United States is concerned much has been debated and written about its future options since President Clinton stepped into the White House. For many he symbolises the break with the American past, with the role of American Presidents who experienced the Second World War and whose foreign policies were influenced accordingly. If this itself were not enough to cast doubt on the maintenance of the Pax Americana and the role of the United States in the world, he arrived with associates carrying different intellectual baggage from all his post-Second World War predecessors, with perhaps the exception of PresidentCarter. The Administration has no commitment in principle to universal free trade (whatever it may do in practice). It has made noises to the effect that in this brave new world, America must come first and that the interests of middle America must take precedence over the State Department and the Pentagon.

How much of the rhetoric will be translated into a more isolationist America is hard to say. The American political system has both the merit and demerit of having much inertia built into its legislative processes. Both Presidents and Congress may often shout, but to no effect. Whatever the outcome in this particular case a lurch toward isolationism by the United States would be a serious matter for the world and ultimately for the United States itself. A retreat into the economics and politics of the inter-war period would be an unmitigated disaster for all.

Is it likely to happen? Probably not. As has been pointed out, Harry Johnson at the outset of the BNAC was writing at the end of an era. The control of monetary policy was handed back to the principal trading nations. There is an analogy here with the end of the Cold War, the end of another longer era. Some of the major players have been handed back a greater degree of control over their political destinies. It is to be hoped that unlike their reaction to apparent control over their economic destinies they will not take themselves so seriously.

The analysis presented suggests some degree of pessimism for world economic outcomes in so far as economic co-operation is likely to become more difficult rather than less. Domestic needs (or what are mistakenly seen as domestic needs) will tend to dominate collective responsibility. These developments will be reinforced by a tendency to re-establish more traditional patterns of economic and political relations (and enmities!). This suggests that where co-operative and mutual benefits are seen, they will be more clearly placed on a narrower basis than on the world canvas, where both motivation and mechanism will prove to be lacking. In economic terms we can see no return to a golden age, rather a rough ride along an upward path.

This conclusion must be underlined by the fact that, as noted at the beginning of this section, we have been analysing the consequences for the major international economic players of the apparent ending of the Cold War. Certainly it is unlikely that the Soviet Union will be restored in the image of the past. But one must not lose sight of Russia's nuclear capability which, in the "wrong hands", could still present a global threat. Communism as such may have passed on. But as will be argued later, the idea that that leads us inevitably toward the triumph of liberal democracy is likely to be at worst untrue and at best a gross exaggeration.

9. The Pattern of Nations (The Developing World)

To begin with, recent analysis suggests that the way in which the share of countries' output in world output is calculated materially underestimates the contribution of the non-OECD[18]. We saw in Table 6 that the US share of world output has fallen by about 50% between 1965 and 1990. This estimate and the others in this Table are based on the conventional method of estimation. The gross domestic product for each country is converted into US dollars at the ruling exchange rate. But as we have already seen, exchange rates may for significant periods depart from their purchasing power parity values. Consequently, exchange rate weighted estimates of income per head may bear little relation to economic reality. To illustrate the point, the depreciation of the yuan, China's currency from 1.7 to the US dollar in 1978 to about 5.5 (at the time of writing) would more than counter-balance the entire growth of China's real economy over this period.

An alternative set of estimates, based on purchasing power parity rates, is given in Table 17. This clearly suggests that the share of world output contributed by the G7 countries, relative to the developing world may be grossly exaggerated. The alternative method reduces the contribution of the G7 from 63% to 46%. While all estimates must be subject to a health warning, and not taken too literally, anecdotal evidence confirms the view that the conventional approach often grossly underestimates the real standard of living of many countries outside the OECD when measurements are made in US dollars and where the basket of goods typically consumed is often very different from that of the industrial world.

At a macro-economic level, this has a number of implications if we take the larger numbers as being indicative. The first is that on the basis of current growth rates, the share of the non-OECD countries is likely to increase rapidly into the next century. Moreover, these increases in share are likely to occur in countries that have so far made few headlines. If we take Asia, for example, after Japan, the economic miracles have been identified with the so-called

[18] I am particularly indebted to Geoffrey Bell for emphasising this point.

Asian Tigers. But in fact, on the basis of Table 17, they account for less than 2½% currently of world output. In absolute terms, they are dwarfed by China and India, and even Brazil alone at present accounts for 3%.

The second is that given these developments in terms of output, there will be a continual growth in the importance of these countries as trading nations. The significance of the GATT discussed earlier in this paper has focussed on the trading relationships between the current big industrial players, North America, the European Union and Japan. But it is clear that in terms of economic benefits for the world as a whole, much has to come from rising living standards in the case of the less developed members of the OECD and the countries outside it.

Table 17
Shares in World Output

INDUSTRIAL COUNTRIES	**Exchange Rate Based Weights**	**PPP-Based Weights**
United States	26.07	22.47
Japan	14.61	7.63
Germany	6.23	4.26
France	4.99	3.50
Italy	4.38	3.39
United Kingdom	4.19	3.45
Canada	2.58	2.16
Other	10.15	7.58
	73.21	**54.44**
DEVELOPING COUNTRIES		
Africa	1.72	4.05
Asia	7.29	17.69
Middle East & Europe	4.28	4.46
Western Hemisphere	4.42	8.21
	17.71	**34.38**
COUNTRIES IN TRANSITION		
Former Soviet Union	7.53	8.31
Central Europe	1.53	2.85
	9.07	**11.18**

To realise these benefits requires a change in attitude and policies on the part of the countries themselves. They must be fully integrated into the world trading system. Unfortunately, for many years after the Second World War, the conventional paradigm for economic development focussed on what might be described as fortress policies. Industrial developments behind protectionist walls were aimed at import substitution. Strict controls were placed on capital imports and exports. In many cases, such as India for example, regulation, state planning and national ownership restricted the working of the free market. Internal competition hardly existed. The ultimate idea, that the butterfly would emerge from the chrysalis did not materialise.

In all parts of this world there has been a change of heart. From South America to South-East Asia, even to some degree in India, a new philosophy has emerged that is encouraging de-regulation of markets, privatisation of enterprise, a greater freedom of capital movements and a greater focus on internal competition. Clearly these developments are unevenly spread throughout the developing world. The pace is different from country to country. Moreover, many of these developments are fragile plants against a background of domestic political uncertainty.

The other side of this coin is the response of the developed industrial world. To achieve the integration of the developing with the developed world requires a political response from the developed countries themselves. As Harry Johnson saw a quarter of a century ago, what the developing world needs is trade not aid - real investment and the opening of domestic markets.

As we have seen recently in the context of the discussion of the North American Free Trade Agreement between the United States, Canada and Mexico, such developments do not come easily. The major countries see their declining share of world output and markets as a sign of weakness, rather than as a perfectly normal and healthy adjustment. They fear the increased competitiveness of the newly industrialising countries. To counter this fear, the benefits of free trade and multilateralism must be kept alive.

Finally, given the size and the potential growth rate of non-OECD output, the developing world will come to play a more significant role in the determination of world output in the short run. The OECD has need to be mindful of its health.

It is impossible in this space to make much more than general comments about the developing world. Despite some similarities between the developing regions there are also material differences. At the beginning of the BNAC there was great optimism about South America and the rush to lend money in the face of the oil price shocks ended in near disaster, both for the countries themselves and for the banks that lent to them. Meanwhile South-East Asia prospered. For a long period, the giants of India and China slumbered. Much sub-Sahara Africa still looks to be without hope. There is much confusion in Russian and Central and Eastern Europe.

Probably the most significant overall development of the next decade in economic terms will be the continual growth and expansion of Asia, including in Asia for this purpose, China and the Indian subcontinent. As can be seen in Table 17, defined in this way, it already accounts for more than a quarter of total world output and a share of world exports of some 30%. The estimates given in Table 17 imply that North America, the European Union and Asia contribute about 70% of world output at the present time. When growth will take place in Latin America, in Russia and the East and Central Europe, the Asian economic region is probably better equipped to make progress than elsewhere.

Asians believe in modernisation, education and skills, and the importation of Western technology. Much of it is developing as a consumer based society, without the prevailing sin of conventional liberal democracy, that the prime function of government is to solve problems at the taxpayers expense. Given current growth rates some estimates suggest that by the end of the decade, Asia will account for something like half the annual increase in world trade.

Much of this will depend on the giants of India and China. As already described, the Indian economy, for many years, has been subject to extensive state planning, state ownership and protectionism. More recently, attempts have been made to de-regulate the economy, combined with effective macro-economic stabilisation policies that have brought inflation into simple figures and enabled the currency to become convertible. India has the advantage at the macro-economic level of a relatively sophisticated administrative and financial system. Its principal difficulty lies in the absence of a strong entrepreneurial culture - although that does not seem to have held back Indian businessmen overseas. However, even compared with China, India's conversion to the ideas that de-regulation and free trade may be essential to more rapid economic growth is comparatively recent (1991). It remains to be seen to what extent further economic reform can be sold to the vested interests that have held India back in the past.

The story of China has become familiar. It begins post-Mao with the decision of the Communist Party in December 1978 to accept proposals for economic reform put forward by Deng Xiaoping. In very general terms, China was to be opened up to the trading world outside and commitment to the historic principles of central planning, state ownership and import substitution reduced. In the years since then and to date, real GDP in China has grown on average at the rate of about 9% a year. Exports as a percentage of GDP have grown from 6% in 1978 to about 15% today, and the percentage is rising.

While recently China's growth rate at some 13% may not be sustainable, the advance over the last 15 years has not represented a simple dash for growth. It was based initially -as are all industrial revolutions - on the developments in the agricultural sector. Whereas hitherto the peasantry were repressed with little encouragement to expand output and raise productivity, the new reforms put money into their pockets. Grain output rose by a third: in six years cotton output trebled, and in eight years real incomes of the farmers grew threefold. Savings needed to finance industrial development were obtained from the primary sector not by brute force, but raising its income level.

Subsequently, the new "open-door" policy was introduced by setting up "special economic zones", three in Guangdong, next door to Hong Kong, and the other in Fugian province. Clearly the success of Guangdong owes much to its proximity to Hong Kong. But more generally, both trade and foreign investment have introduced competition into the Chinese economy. Some estimates suggest that with the rapid growth of small business, the states' share of total industrial output will have fallen to 25% by the year 2000. The sheer scale of China means that, with a continuation of the growth rates of the 1980s, early next century, China in absolute terms could be the second largest economy in the world after the United States.

What could happen to prevent this?

While China has clearly been relatively successful with regard to its micro-economic reforms, it has been less successful at creating the financial infrastructure that development requires. The result is a clear danger of interruptions to the growth process being brought about by bouts of inflation and monetary instability as we have seen in the past. In this respect, China lacks the sophistication of India and the diaspora Chinese. A step in this direction toward a more capitalist financial economy would be desirable.

This issue is linked with the wider political uncertainty that surrounds China. All revolutions, whether of the right or the left, have their opponents, particularly those who have strong vested interests in the *status quo*. It is unclear what will follow the death of Den Xiaoping. How far the Communist Party is prepared to go in creating and accepting capitalist institutions and mores as part of the price of continued economic growth is equally unclear.

Politics may yet overcome economics on the road to a higher standard of living.

It has been argued that economic development and reform in China has been possible, but unlike the former Soviet Union, the Chinese are attempting one thing at a time. In the Soviet Union and its former satellites, we are seeing attempts to re-fashion the economic and political system at the same time. Russia is of course the supreme example. It remains a serious problem with the capability of becoming a major political force. While it is possible to argue, as earlier, that in a significant sense the Cold War as we have known it is over, this does not eliminate the possibility that Russia, together with a new sphere of influence outside its borders, will not in the future constitute a political force to be reckoned with. The failure of economic reform may lead to a political formation that will make the former Western Allies distinctly uncomfortable.

This highlights the need on the part of the Western alliance to be concerned about economic developments in the old Soviet Union and its former sphere of influence. A theme that emerges from several parts of this essay is the need to encourage free trade and economic growth in the world as a whole as a key part in the process of ensuring political stability and security.

Development and growth in Russia and its neighbours will be difficult to achieve. The potential is enormous, particularly with regard to raw materials and oil. Already, in certain materials such as aluminium, Russian output is significant. However, it is likely that, given the political uncertainty and the size of the problem of privatisation, the principal significance of the area in economic terms will be postponed until well into the next century.

10. The End of History - or More of the Same?

At a simplistic level the ending of the Cold War may be interpreted as the triumph of capitalism over communism. There is little doubt that the economics of Communism (with a capital C) have been an unmitigated disaster for the countries of the Eastern European bloc. It is also hard to dispute that the political bouleversement that we have seen, dramatically represented by the collapse of the Berlin Wall and the disintegration of the Soviet Union, has fundamental economic roots. One can agree with the power that Marx attributed to economic forces without agreeing with his predictions, which have turned out to be palpably false.

But it still leaves open the question as to how we can expect the countries outside Eastern Europe to develop in terms of economic organisation. The view that one form of economic organisation has triumphed absolutely over another will probably turn out to be grossly oversimplified. It finds its extreme statement in the context of the well known thesis of Francis Fukuyama - we have reached the end of history.[19]

The argument is as follows. Praying in aid philosophers and economists as far apart as Hegel and Marx, history is seen as a process that leads to some determinate outcome or equilibrium result in terms of political and economic organisation. For Marx the inevitable outcome for history and its last resting place was the Communist state. For Hegel it was effectively the triumph of liberal democracy. Thus the historical process for both was not open ended but had a final outcome. For Fukuyama, the end of the Hegelian process is at hand:

> "The most remarkable development of the last quarter of the twentieth century has been the revelation of enormous weaknesses at the core of the world's seemingly strong dictatorships, whether they be of the military-authoritarian Right or the communist-totalitarian Left. From Latin America to Eastern Europe, from the Soviet Union to the Middle East and Asia, strong governments have been failing over the last two decades.

---

[19] Francis Fukuyama *The End of History and the Last Man*, Penguin Books 1992

> And while they have not given way in all cases to stable liberal democracies, liberal democracy remains the only coherent political aspiration that spans different regions and cultures around the globe. In addition, liberal principles in economics - the "free market" - have spread and have succeeded in producing unprecedented levels of material prosperity both in industrially developed countries that had been at the close of World War II part of the impoverished Third World." (Fukujama *op cit* p. xiii)

There are elements of truth in this view - attitudes towards markets in the OECD have been shifting significantly over the last twenty years. Also what is probably true, by implication, is that there has been an overarching economic philosophy, call it socialism or what you will, called upon to remedy all ills, which is no longer believed in except by a small minority. The status of, and perception of, the effectiveness of governments and government institutions has undoubtedly declined in both the West and the East. However, the conclusion that this is leading to the universal adoption of something called liberal democracy in both the political and economic spheres is at best a gross exaggeration and at worst, misleading.

The argument fails to recognise a number of significant issues. The first is that it is not clear what is meant by "liberal democracy" - or alternatively, however we define it, it comes in many different forms. The idea that the Asian Tigers, followed by China will converge on something we identify as a European/Anglo-American form of liberal democracy is hard to believe. Political structures are likely to continue to differ widely between countries and cultures. The notion that the substantial part of the world that is devoted to Islam will in the foreseeable future reflect the characteristics of Western liberal democracies is especially hard to take seriously.

Secondly, while it is probably true that the concept of an overarching socialism has disappeared for the foreseeable future, it still remains unclear that there is universal agreement in the Western world as to where the line between government and the private market place is to be drawn. This reflects the constant and continuing conflict between the activity of what we may describe as political markets on the one hand and of economic markets on the other. The former deals in votes and promises, the latter with the supply and demand for real economic resources. The British economic commentator and former UK Ambassador to the US, Peter Jay, sought several years ago to identify the root cause of inflation in Western societies in the reconciliation of these markets - political promises *vis-à-vis* the availability of real economic resources.[20] As we saw earlier, the prospect is for a continuous and rising demand on the behalf of citizens for resources to be provided by the State. There is no reason to believe that this chronic source of tension has suddenly disappeared. Moreover, the balance between the market and the State shifts in response to economic performance. When the latter weakens, the demand for State intervention rises, and *vice versa*.

The conclusion from all this is probably that history has not come to an end in Fukuyama's sense, despite the collapse of communism in Eastern Europe. Neither have we witnessed an overwhelming triumph of liberal democracy whether in economic or political terms. The somewhat mundane conclusion is that, shorn of the socialist fantasies that have been manifestly discredited on practical grounds, the West is committed to some form of "managed capitalism" over the next decade. Its precise nature will clearly vary from country to country and culture to culture. Its character is also likely to vary with the course of economic events. From time to time the emphasis will be on the management and from time to time on the capitalism. What will all this mean for us in the longer run?

In June 1930, in the midst of the slump, Maynard Keynes gave a lecture in Madrid entitled "Economic Possibilities for our Grandchildren". He began:

> "We are suffering just now from a bad attack of economic pessimism. It is common to hear people say that the epoch of enormous economic progress which characterised the nineteenth century is over; that the rapid improvement in the standard of life is now going to slow down - at any rate in Great Britain; that a decline in prosperity is more likely than an improvement in the decade which lies ahead of us".[21]

The optimism that Keynes expresses echoes that of Ricardo of over 150 years ago, who looked forward to an inevitable state of bliss that would result in the rate of interest being driven down to zero as capital became a free good. Ricardo's vision was flawed because he failed to appreciate the way in which

[20] P Jay, "Employment, Inflation and Politics", 6th Wincott Memorial Lecture, *IEA Occasional Paper*, 1976

[21] J M Keynes, "Economic Possibilities for our Grandchildren", 1930, *The Collected Writings of John Maynard Keynes, Volume IX Essays in Persuasion*, Macmillan St Martin's Press published for the Royal Economic Society, 1972, p. 321

technical progress would continue to maintain a positive, real marginal productivity of capital, as Marx failed to anticipate the flexibility of ownership under capitalism. Keynes said, further, that:

> "The *pace* (his italics) at which we can reach our destination of economic bliss will be governed by four things - our power to control population, our determination to avoid wars and civil dissensions, our willingness to entrust to science the direction of those matters which are properly the concern of science, and the rate of accumulation as fixed by the margin between our production and our consumption; of which the last will easily look after itself, given the first three". (Keynes *op cit* p. 331)

Keynes made much of two issues. The first was that the problems being faced by the economic world were essentially problems caused by success rather than failure. The existence of unemployment, associated at the same time with technological progress, was a

> "temporary phase of maladjustment. All this means in the long run *that mankind is solving its economic problem* (his italics)." (Keynes *op cit* p. 325)

The second is his emphasis on the power of compound interest:

> "The modern age opened, I think, with the accumulation of capital which began in the sixteenth century. I believe ..... that this was initially due to the rise of prices, and the profits to which that led, which resulted from the treasure of gold and silver which Spain brought from the New World into the Old. From that time until today the power of accumulation by compound interest, which seems to have been sleeping for many generations, was reborn and renewed its strength. And the power of compound interest over two hundred years is such as to stagger the imagination." (Keynes *op cit* p. 323)

He went on to point out that,

> "If capital increases, say, two per cent per annum, the capital equipment of the world will have increased by a half in twenty years, and seven and a half times in a hundred years. Think of this in terms of material things - houses, transport and the like." (Keynes *op cit,* p. 325)

The history of output per head in the USA, Canada and the United Kingdom since 1920 is set out in Table 18. We can see that on average over the whole period output per head in the US has risen at an average rate of 1.9% per annum, in Canada at a rate of 2.2% and in the United Kingdom 1.7%. If we take the post-War period defined as 1950 to 1989, the figures are 2%, 2.6% and 2.2% respectively. It can be seen that variations between the decades of the post-War period have been relatively small and it may be suggested that something very odd has got to happen for realised rates of growth over the next twenty years to be either dramatically greater or dramatically less than these numbers. Not the end of history: probably more of the same.

Table 18
GDP/GNP: IInternational Comparisons
annual growth rate per capita
selected periods 1913-1989

	Canada	United Kingdom	United States
1913-29	0.7	0.3	1.7
1929-50	1.8	1.2	1.8
1950-60	1.9	2.4	1.4
1960-70	3.4	2.2	2.8
1970-80	3.0	1.6	1.6
1980-89	2.3	2.6	2.1

*1913-1950 = GNP
1950-1989 = GDP

Source: US Department of Commerce, USA, Bureau of the Census
US Bureau of Economic Analysis, Long Term Economic Growth
OECD National Accounts 1960-89

11. Epilogue

Prediction is fraught with danger. The principal concern of this paper has been to raise issues rather than predict. Even less has it preoccupied itself with offering solutions to the issues raised. Nevertheless, however imperfect the maps we use to guide ourselves, we need them, not because they will eventually get us to some desirable destination. They are necessary if only to provide some rational basis for the decisions we make today. Some vision is required, even if unanticipated events may cause it to be no more than a mirage. This paper has suggested a number of elements that might be put together as part of such a vision.

Rapid economic growth of a kind seen by the major industrial countries in the Age of Prosperity is a thing of the past. Even allowing for the fact that there is still a significant statistical gap between the United States and the rest, all these countries are probably close enough to the world technical growth frontier to prevent any dramatic changes in underlying growth rates in the foreseeable future. For these countries, there will be a continual reduction in the significance of manufacturing industry both as a proportion of gross domestic product and as an employer of people.

The path of technology, associated with the changes in industrial structure are already creating and will continue to create problems of labour market adjustment for the industrial countries, particularly in the European Union. In general, the need for the major industrial countries to occupy the high ground of technical advance, beyond the mass production culture on which they have built in the past will put an increasing premium on skill based occupations. There will be a major problem in the next decade and beyond in coming to terms with the fact that it is only through supply side changes that unemployment rates in the OECD can be materially reduced. There will be a strong temptation to put in place "artificial" measures of job creation that in the longer run will only aggravate rather than help the problem.

Provided that political storms do not throw them off course, significant growth is to be expected in Asia, possibly in South America, and less likely in Russia and its sphere of influence. But the general effect will be for countries outside the OECD to increase materially their share of world output and trade by the end of the century and beyond. This must be seen as a desirable and normal course of events as countries pan through the different stages of economic maturity and legitimately aspire to the standards of living of those who have gone before. Their progress must not be seen as a threat but as an opportunity to share in the creation of markets.

This process has fundamental links with the development of trade. If the response of the developed countries is an instinctive lurch toward protectionism, and in the case of the United States, isolationism, the effect could be disastrous. As was pointed out earlier, the consequences of protectionism are not simply economic: they are intensely political.

Steady progress in the trading world requires a stable financial environment. It has been argued that inflation is not a normal state of affairs for the industrial countries and that the experience of the 1970s and 1980s was exceptional. The outlook for inflation over the recent decade depends crucially on whether the public has been convinced of the costs of an inflationary world. Most of the short run factors suggest that inflation should stay subdued for the rest of this century at least, unless, as has happened before, the world is subject to another unanticipated shock.

Severe deflation in the industrial world is unlikely if only for the persistent pressure to increase public expenditure which raises all the same issues that were discussed by Harry Johnson twenty-five years ago. Public sector expenditure, or more particularly the means of financing it, remains the principal threat to low inflation. The pressures arising from the costs of health, welfare and retirement benefits among the major industrial players, require a radical shift in the approach to service delivery over the next twenty-five years if expectations are to be consistent with stable public finances.

Public attitudes toward international competitiveness in the major industrialised countries have not caught up with the decline in relative competitiveness. There is a serious danger that regulatory procedures will be used to restrict market performance on ideological grounds and the costs imposed on business and commerce. This is likely to be the case across a wide range of commercial activities including public utilities, financial services and environmental issues.

The end of the Cold War has posed a number of new questions for the major players on the world economic scene. The future of the Economic Union, the blueprint for which was conceived in other times has all the hallmarks of an outdated brief. The whole question of what Europe will be is in the melting pot. The re-unification of Germany has created a new heavyweight to place on the scales of power. It is not clear that its future lies in a wholehearted commitment to a Europe of the post-war making. Japan faces not only a need to reconsider the way it does business, but also a need to determine its identity in changed circumstances. Finally, the United States must decide to what extent it will maintain openness to the world outside and continue to try and keep something of the Pax American in place.

The ending of the Cold War cannot simply be seen as the triumph of liberal democracy over communism. At best, it has demonstrated the superiority of the market system over collectivism. The recognition of this conclusion is affecting economic behaviour from Beijing to Buenos Aires. But even in the case of the industrial countries there is no clear agreement as to the balance between the private market sector and the state. For these countries, some form of managed capitalism is likely, but even here there are differences in its interpretation. With regard to political development in Russia and China, their response to economic reform is even more difficult to predict.

Nothing is inevitable, which is why prediction is so difficult. The future is not written in stone. What we will see as we enter the next century and beyond will depend on how governments in both economic and political terms respond to the issues discussed in this paper.

Sponsoring Organisations

The British-North American Research Association was inaugurated in December 1969. Its primary purpose is to sponsor research on British-North American economic relations in association with the British-North American Committee. Publications of the British-North American Research Association as well as publications of the British-North American Committee are available from the Association's office, Grosvenor Gardens House, 35-37 Grosvenor Gardens, London SW1W 0BS (Tel. 071-828 6644). The Association is registered as a charity and is governed by a Council under the chairmanship of Sir David Plastow.

The National Planning Association is an independent, private, non-profit, non-political organisation that carries on research and policy formulation in the public interest. NPA was founded during the Great Depression of the 1930s when conflicts among the major economic groups – business, labour, agriculture – threatened to paralyse national decisionmaking on the critical issues confronting American society. NPA is dedicated to the task of getting these diverse groups to work together to narrow areas of controversy and broaden areas of agreement as well as to map out specific programs for action in the best traditions of a functioning democracy. Such democratic and decentralised planning, NPA believes, involves the development of effective government and private policies and programs not only by official agencies but also through the independent initiative and cooperation of the main private sector groups concerned.

To this end, NPA brings together influential and knowledgeable leaders from business, labour, agriculture, and the applied and academic professions to serve on policy committees. These committees identify emerging problems confronting the nation at home and abroad and seek to develop and agree upon policies and programs for coping with them. The research and writing for these committees are provided by NPA's professional staff and, as required, by outside experts.

In addition, NPA's professional staff undertakes research through its central or "core" programs designed to provide data and ideas for policy-makers and planners in government and the private sector. These activities include research on national goals and priorities, productivity and economic growth, welfare and dependency problems, employment and human resource needs, and technological change; analyses and forecasts of changing international realities and their implications for U.S. policies; and analyses of important new economic, social, and political realities confronting American society.

In developing its staff capabilities, NPA has increasingly emphasised two related qualifications. First is the interdisciplinary knowledge required to understand the complex nature of many real-life problems. Second is the ability to bridge the gap between theoretical or highly technical research and the practical needs of policymakers and planners in government and the private sector.

Malcolm R. Lovell, Jr., is President and Chief Executive Officer.

NPA publications, including those of the British-North American Committee, can be obtained from the Association's office, 1424 16th Street, N.W., Suite 700, Washington, D.C. 20036 (Tel. 202-884 7631).

The C.D. Howe Institute is an independent, non-partisan, non-profit research and education institution. It carries out and makes public independent analyses and critiques of economic policy issues, and translates scholarly research into choices for action by governments and the private sector.

The Institute was established in 1973 by the merger of the C.D. Howe Memorial Foundation and the Private Planning Association of Canada (PPAC). The Foundation had been created in 1961 to memorialise the late Right Honorable C.D. Howe, who served Canada in many elected capacities between 1935 and 1957, including Minister of Trade and Commerce. The PPAC was a unique forum created in 1958 by leaders of business and labour for the purpose of carrying out research and educational activities on economic policy issues.

While its focus is national and international, the Institute recognises that Canada is composed of regions, each of which may have a particular perspective on policy issues and different concepts of what should be national priorities.

A Board of Directors is responsible for the Institute's general direction and for safeguarding its independence. The President is the chief executive and is responsible for formulating and carrying out policy, directing research and selecting staff. In order to promote the flexibility and relevance of its work, the

Institute's high quality professional staff is intentionally kept small and is supplemented with a number of scholars and compatible institutions.

Participation in the Institute's activities is encouraged from business, organised labour, trade associations, and the professions. Through objective examinations of different points of view, the Institute seeks to increase public understanding of policy issues and to contribute to the public decisionmaking process.

Tom Kierans is President and Treasurer.

The Institute's offices are located at: P.O. Box 1621, Calgary, Alberta T2P 2L7; and 125 Adelaide Street East, Toronto, Ontario M5C 1L7 (Tel. in Toronto, 416-865 1904).

Publications of the British-North American Committee

BN-39
The World Economy: Trends and Prospects for the Next Decade
by Sir James Ball, June 1994 (£10.00, U.S.$15.00)

BN-38
The Question of Saving
by Harold Rose, March 1991 (£4.00, U.S.$8.00)

BN-37
On Preserving Shared Values: A Committee Statement on the 40th Anniversary of the North Atlantic Treaty
May 1989 (£1.25, U.S.$2.00)

BN-36
The GATT Negotiations 1986-1990: Origins, Issues and Prospects
by Sidney Golt, November 1988 (£6.00, U.S.$10.00)

BN-35
Stiffening the Sinews of the Nations: Economic Infrastructure in the United States, United Kingdom, and Canada
by Simon Webley, December 1985 (£4.00, U.S.$6.00)

BN-34
The Process of Innovation
by Nuala Swords-Isherwood, October 1984 (£5.00, U.S.$8.00)

BN-33
Governments and Multinationals: Policies in the Developed Countries
by A.E. Safarian, December 1983 (£4.00, U.S.$8.00)

BN-32
Trade Issues in the Mid 1980s
by Sidney Golt, with a Committee Policy Statement, October 1982 (£3.50, U.S.$7.00)

BN-31
The Newly Industrializing Countries: Adjusting to Success
by Neil McMullen, November 1982 (£3.50, U.S.$7.00)

BN-30
Conflicts of National Laws with International Business Activity: Issues of Extraterritoriality
by A.H. Hermann, August 1982 (£3.00, U.S.$6.00)

BN-29
Industrial Innovation in the United Kingdom, Canada and the United States
by Kerry Schott, July 1981 (£2.25, U.S.$5.00)

BN-28
Flexible Exchange Rates and International Business
by John M. Blin, Stuart I. Greenbaum and Donald P. Jacobs, December 1981 (£3.00, U.S.$8.00)

BN-27
A Trade Union View of US Manpower Policy
by William W. Winpisinger, April 1980 (£1.75, U.S.$3.00)

BN-26
A Positive Approach to the International Economic Order, Part II: Non-Trade Issues
by Alasdair MacBean and V.N. Balasubramanyam, May 1980 (£2.25, U.S.$5.00)

BN-25
New Patterns of World Mineral Development
by Raymond F. Mikesell, September 1979 (£2.25, U.S.$5.00)

BN-24
Inflation Is a Social Malady
by Carl E. Beigie, March 1979 (£2.00, U.S.$4.00)

BN-23
A Positive Approach to the International Economic Order, Part I: Trade & Structural Adjustment
by Alasdair MacBean, October 1978 (£1.75, U.S.$3.00)

BN-22
The GATT Negotiations 1973-79: The Closing Stage
by Sidney Golt, with a Committee Policy Statement, May 1978 (£1.50, U.S.$3.00)

BN-21
Skilled Labour Supply Imbalances: The Canadian Experience
by William Dodge, November 1977 (£1.50, U.S.$3.00)

BN-20
The Soviet Impact on World Grain Trade
by D. Gale Johnson, May 1977 (£1.75, U.S.$3.00)

BN-19
Mineral Development in the Eighties: Prospects and Problems
A report prepared by a group of Committee members with a Statistical Annex by Sperry Lea, November 1976 (£1.50, U.S.$3.00)

BN-18
Skilled Labour Shortages in the United Kingdom: With Particular Reference to the Engineering Industry
by Gerry Eastwood, October 1976 (£1.50, U.S.$3.00)

BN-17
Higher Oil Prices: Worldwide Financial Implications
A Policy Statement by the British-North American Committee and a Research Report by Sperry Lea, October 1975 (£1.50, U.S.$3.00)

BN-16
Completing the GATT: Toward New International Rules to Govern Export Controls
by C. Fred Bergsten, October 1974 (80p, U.S.$2.00)

BN-15
Foreign Direct Investment in the United States: Opportunities and Impediments
by Simon Webley, September 1974 (80p, U.S.$2.00)

BN-14
The GATT Negotiations, 1973-75: A Guide to the Issues
by Sidney Golt, April 1974 (£1.00, U.S.$2.00)

BN-13
Problems of Economic Development in the Caribbean
by David Powell, compiled from a study by Irene Hawkins, November 1973 (80p, U.S.$2.00)

BN-12
The European Approach to Worker-Management Relationships
by Innis Macbeath, October 1973 (£1.00, U.S.$2.50)

BN-11
An International Grain Reserve Policy
by Timothy Josling, July 1973 (40p, U.S.$1.00)

BN-10
Man and His Environment
by Harry G. Johnson, August 1973 (40p, U.S.$1.00)

BN-9
Prospective Changes in the World Trade and Monetary System: A Comment
A Statement by the BNAC, October 1972 (30p, U.S.$0.75)

BN-8
Multinational Corporations in Developed Countries: A Review of Rekcent Research and Policy Thinking
by Sperry Lea and Simon Webley, March 1973 (80p, U.S.$2.00)

BN-7
Sterling, European Monetary Unification, and the International Monetary System
by Richard N. Cooper, March 1972 (40p, U.S.$1.00)

BN-6
Multinational Corporations and British Labour: A Review of Attitudes and Responses
by John Gennard, January 1972 (80p, U.S.$2.00)

Issues Paper-3
Unfinished Tasks: The New International Trade Theory and the Post-Uruguay Round Challenge
by F.M. Scherer and Richard S. Belous May 1994 (£6.00, U.S.$9.00)

Issues Paper-2
The Changing World of Finance and Its Problems
by Harold Rose, March 1993 (£6.00, U.S.$9.00)

Issues Paper-1
Continuing Education and Training of the Workforce
by Frederick W. Crawford and Simon Webley, November 1992 (£9.00, U.S.$16.00)

Occasional Paper-7
Demographic Currents: Trends and Issues that Face the United States, the United Kingdom and Canada
by Richard S. Belous, with a Foreword by Thomas H.B. Symons, September 1991 (£5.00, U.S.$8.00)

Occasional Paper-6
Man and His Environment
by the late Harry G. Johnson, with a Commentary by Frances Cairncross, June 1990 (£5.00, U.S.$8.00)

Occasional Paper-5
New Departures in Industrial Relations: Developments in the U.S., the U.K. and Canada
April 1988 (£4.00, U.S.$7.00)

Occasional Paper-4
Tensions in U.S.-E.E.C. Relations: The Agriculture Issue
by Sir Richard Butler and Thomas Saylor, December 1986 (£2.00, U.S.$3.00)

Publications of the British-North American Committee

Occasional Paper-3
Managing Product Innovation
The views of five BNAC members: Carrol Bolen, Ken Durham, Walter Light, Chester Sadlow, and Viscount Weir, October 1984 (£1.50, U.S.$2.00)

Occasional Paper-2
Managing the Response to Industrial Decline
by Joseph L. bower, September 1984 (£1.50, U.S.$2.00)

Occasional Paper-1
New Investment in Basic Industries
Prepared by a Committee Task Force, June 1979 (60p, U.S.$1.00)

Publications of the British-North American Committee are available from:

In Great Britain and Europe
BRITISH-NORTH AMERICAN RESEARCH ASSOCIATION
Grosvenor Gardens House
35-37 Grosvenor Gardens
London SW1W 0BS

Tel: 071-828 6644
Fax: 071-828 5830

In the United States of America
NATIONAL PLANNING ASSOCIATION
1424 16th Street NW, Suite 700
Washington, DC 20036

Tel: 202-884 7631
Fax: 202-797 5516

In Canada
C.D. HOWE INSTITUTE
125 Adelaide Street East
Toronto, Ontario M5C 1L7

Tel: 416-865 1904
Fax: 416-865 1866